I0159034

LONG WAY HOME

Help Can Come From

Unlikely Places

George Samerjan

Copyright © 2014 the North Chatham Company, Ltd.
All rights reserved.
ISBN-13: 9780615949116
ISBN-10: 0615949118
Library of Congress Control Number: 2014903830
North Chatham Company, Ltd.

DEDICATION

*For my wife, Joy, who was there for me during my long way
home after the Vietnam War.*
George Samerjan

CONTENTS

ACKNOWLEDGMENTS

The author gratefully thanks the following for their help, support, and encouragement.

John Silbersack - agent and reviewer who provided invaluable counsel before and during the writing of this novel

And Teddy and Happy - who patiently abided during writing days

PROLOGUE

I'm Henry Two Pines. It falls to me to tell you the story. I knew Brian, and Johnnie True Blood, and then Barbara, and little Katie. I witnessed parts of what happened, heard about others, and some parts came to me. You know how that is when you're passing along a story. You keep running it through your mind and parts drop off and parts get added, and you lose track of what you saw or what you think you saw.

It seems to me that lots of folks can get value from the divine rescue of Sergeant McAfee - Brian. I did. Me and Angie partly raised him along with Johnnie True Blood, but that's getting ahead.

The story starts when the Army brought Johnnie True Blood home to me and Angie in a flag draped coffin; back to the deep woods of the Adirondacks.

This story had to happen here in the Adirondacks. There's a bold stillness that can come upon you up here; stillness at dusk in a clearing, a pause by a creek or under the shadow of a ponderous cloud. Quiet. Stillness. Rising in the early hours. Listening to the coyotes on one side of the lake singing to those on the other. Feeling their songs but not knowing the words. You sense the eyes of a mountain lion on you but can't see him. Looking up to the Milky Way and seeing that bright corridor of stars leading off across the sky. The sense that something so much bigger than you is present right next to you if you could only see it. That's what this story is about.

CHAPTER 1

HOME AT LAST

TOO HEAVY A BURDEN

*S*taff Sergeant Brian McAfee knelt next to Sergeant Johnnie True Blood *in the shadow of the burning HUM-V on the desolate dirt track in Afghanistan. The squad formed a perimeter though no Taliban were in sight. Johnnie was dying and there was nothing that Brian, Tiny, or the others could do but ease his pain. Brian nodded his agreement to Tiny. The second injection of morphine coursed through Johnnie's bloodstream to his brain. Johnnie's lips curled from grimace to smile. Brian bent low placing his ear to Johnnie True Blood's lips.*

"My dog tags, get them to Henry Two Pines," Johnnie whispered. "They may fight over my body. Family stuff."

Brian nodded, reached to the chain around Johnnie True Blood's neck and removed one of the two dog tags.

"I will."

"Keep tap dancing, Mac."

Johnnie struggled to breath.

"I'll be seeing you."

With that, Johnnie was gone.

1

Staff Sergeant Brian McAfee pulled down the front of his wide brimmed hat shielding his eyes from the dust and pebbles in the downdraft from the Black Hawk's rotor blades. Grains of sand and dust stung his sun tanned cheeks, and clung to his sweat soaked fatigues. Through the pale brown dust he watched the medics labor with the long, black body bag. Despite the heat of the day a chill went down Brian's spine. Reverently, the medics laid the young sergeant's corpse onto the floor of the helicopter. The crew chief secured it, and then turned looking back outside at McAfee. Words between the two were unnecessary. They had both done this too many times before.

Brian felt as if a large, cold, greasy stone had settled into his stomach. The rotor sped faster and then angled forward causing the ship to lift nose down and pick up speed. To Brian it was as if Johnnie really wasn't dead. This was some kind of practical joke of his and Johnnie would unzip the bag from the inside, lean out of the departing bird, and wave with a great flourish that he had somehow gamed the system and was going home - alive. The Blackhawk became a black spot in the heavens, and then disappeared from view. Brian walked away from the LZ, through the Claymore mines and barbed wire, and up the slope. Brian paused, looking back at where the IED had been planted barely outside their wire. He cursed, and spat on the foreign soil.

Brian slouched in a flimsy aluminum and plastic lawn chair on the patio behind his one story ranch house. Drops of Bourbon spilled on his two day growth of beard as he raised the square bottle to his lips, swallowed the warm, bitter whiskey, and then rested the bottle in his lap. Looking over his left shoulder at the window to Barbara's room he noticed that the light was out meaning that Katie had been tucked in. Katie slept with Barbara now, and Brian occupied his daughter's room. Barbara changed the rules of the family and Brian had no strength to resist.

House rules, no drinking in front of Katie. Fine, she was asleep. Brian took another, long, hard pull on the Bourbon in a vain attempt to coax sleep. He knew what he was doing wouldn't work, but it was the only plan he had. He wouldn't get sleep, but eventually he would pass out. He sat in darkness staring off past the distant street lamps into the night. For an instant the yellow lights reminded him of the outpost in Afghanistan where he and his squad had jury-rigged lights on the perimeter.

Presently, reason intruded. He was home. He knew that. His forearms were scarred where shrapnel from an RPG had nicked him. The others in the HUM-V hadn't been that lucky. He could still hear their screams before death sucked the living breath from their lungs, and he and the others zipped them into body bags, and carried the ugly secret that each of them was glad it hadn't been them - that time.

Behind him he heard Barbara's breath as she paused in the doorway leading from the house to the patio. Heavy. Angry.

He heard the screen door slowly open – slowly and quietly. He heard Barbara's bare foot steps on the cement patio. Her presence behind him annoyed Brian. She knew better than to come up behind him without making noise, yet she insisted on doing it. The hair on his neck bristled, and his shoulder muscles tensed.

Oh God, just leave me alone and let me get blasted in peace and fucking quiet and go to bed.

He heard her take a folded up lawn chair from its place against the wall and open it.

Oh, fuck, now what? Jesus, what the fuck do I have to listen to now?

The sound of the aluminum tube scraping against the cement further annoyed Brian as his wife moved closer.

"And?"

"And, what?" Barbara said.

"You're here," Brian said without looking at his wife.

"Brian," Barbara said firmly, "Don't forget. You have an interview in the morning."

"Fine."

"Do you mean that?"

"Barbara, just let it go. Please."

Brian shook his head, and slowly raised the bottle.

Barbara rose from her chair, stepped to Brian, and reached out for the bottle.

"You ought to go to sleep. Be ready for the interview." Her eyes pleaded.

"Try."

Brian's eyes squinted in anger. He pulled the bottle away from Barbara's reach.

"Just go to bed and leave me alone."

He paused.

"Please."

For an instant they almost connected.

Brian gazed back across the dark lawn toward the street lights.

Barbara turned to walk away and then turned back.

"We can't go on like this!"

"Oh, for Christ's sake would you just give it a rest," Brian said shaking his head.

He rose abruptly from the chair causing it to tumble across the cement like a duck shot in flight somersaulting to the earth. Brian walked away from Barbara into the night.

Barbara ran to a spot ahead of Brian and stopped in his path. Brian tried to continue but Barbara moved in front of him.

"You've got to talk to me!"

"No, Barb, I don't. I don't have to do a fucking thing. I had to do what they told me to do for a year in Iraq and a year in Afghanistan, but I don't have to do anything anymore."

Brian took another swig, and then pointed down at his heavily scarred knees.

"I'm a civilian, Babe, I've got my freedom back. After humping those goddamn hills I don't have any knees left. They couldn't use me anymore. It takes me fifteen minutes to get out of bed in the morning. Wasn't fit for duty."

Brian turned in a circle with his arms outstretched.

"So here I am, Babe. Your loving husband back to you."

The expression on Brian's face changed from bitterness to sorrow.

"Please, Babe, just leave me alone tonight."

"What makes tonight any different? It's the same every night. When is it going to change? You've got to talk to someone."

"Who?"

Brian laughed.

"I was lucky I survived the Warrior Transition unit. Once a week rap session with a nurse and then a bag full of fucking pills so downing you out you couldn't walk, shit, or talk. Another fucking week in that place I would have hung myself."

Brian's tone turned hostile.

"Those fucking stateside noncoms taking shots at us, like we were faking? Faking! I'll show you faking!"

Brian lifted up his polo shirt revealing the lateral scar across his belly where an AK-47 round had scalloped out skin, and the round scar on his right bicep where another AK-47 round had cleanly penetrated his muscle.

"Don't shout, you'll upset the neighbors."

"Oh, the fucking neighbors. How many of them went? How many of those sleeping mother fuckers even knew we were there? They couldn't find Afghanistan on a map!"

Barbara looked to the adjoining houses, and then back to Brian.

"Answer me? How many of them went? None of them. Not one fucking one of them. I don't give a shit about upsetting those assholes."

Brian took a deep breath.

"Babe, just leave me the fuck alone. Please."

He took another deep breath.

"I'm begging you, Babe. For whatever the fuck we had, just leave me alone."

"You're killing yourself!"

She stared at the bottle.

Brian laughed menacingly.

"Al Qaeda didn't get me. The Taliban didn't get me. Sunnis and Shia didn't get me. The fucking IEDs didn't get me." He waved his finger at Barbara. "Almost, but not quite, so I don't think Mister Jack Daniels is going to get me."

Brian looked at the label on the bottle, smiled, and then looked back at Barbara.

Barbara stared at Brian for a moment, and then walked quickly to the house.

Brian went back to the lawn chair, righted it, and drank until he passed out. He didn't hear the bottle fall from his grasp. It shattered against the patio in the middle of the night casting shards of glass in all directions.

Brian heard a voice. Then, he recognized Barbara's voice. Slowly, he opened his eyes to see Barbara above him and Katie standing slightly behind her mother. Somehow he had gotten into the house. He saw fresh scratches on his legs but didn't remember getting them. Brian was sprawled across Katie's bed wearing only his boxers.

"Brian," Barbara said firmly waiting for Brian to focus. She sighed, shook her head, and then continued.

"Don't forget. You have an interview."

Brian caught sight of Katie's pink tennis shoes before she was pulled abruptly away. He wanted to rise, to go to Katie, and to hug her, but he knew that Barbara would stand in his way. He wasn't fit to be a father anymore.

"I still love you, Daddy" Katie said as she was quickly ushered from sight.

"Mommy, why don't you love Daddy anymore?"

Brian dropped his head into his hands and sobbed as hard and deep as he had the first time he'd seen American soldiers die. Brian forced his hands against his eyes until his eyeballs hurt.

His arthritic knees hobbled his gait as he stumbled across the floor. He slapped his hand against the wall in anger at his frailties.

He made it into the bathroom and leaned against the cold, white porcelain sink. He bowed his head before the mirror.

"Snap out of it, you're home now, the war is over. Yeah, get over it."

A wave of nausea swept down his gullet. He leaned toward the commode spewing yellow bile from deep within him. Three times his gut contracted forcing more bile onto the commode and the bathroom floor.

"Aw, fuck."

Slowly, he raised his head, moved toward the faucet, and swished water around in his mouth to clear the taste of his vomit. He shook his head, wiped tears from his eyes with a towel, brushed his long brown hair from his eyes, and stared at his reflection in the mirror.

Had they perhaps sent him home in a flag draped box, and then awakened him just enough to return him to his family with a 'Here he is, Mrs. McAfee. A little worse for the wear, but he's all yours now.'

Maybe Johnnie True Blood was the lucky one? There sure as hell wasn't any pain wherever Johnnie was. Was that the deal all along? Fight your ass off for god and country? And then spent, shot, and out of hope they drop you back where you started with bus fare to our point of origin and the thanks of a grateful nation? What was he supposed to do now? Climb back in the box and wait for the burial honors detail to blow taps?

Raising his left hand, straightening his index finger and pulling back his thumb, he brought the tip of his finger to his temple and knew what he must do that day. It was the day. It had finally come to this. There was sweetness to this.

No need of shower or shave. Brian returned to Katie's room, shuffled in a partly opened suitcase for trousers and a shirt. He dressed quickly, went to the garage and unlocked a metal wall locker. Inside was a padlocked tackle box. He reached for the chain around his neck to the dog tags he still wore. With them was a key. It unlocked the box. The .45 automatic was cold, heavy, and reassuring in his hand. He never cared for the Beretta he had been issued. He went old school and bought an M1911 .45 on the black market and carried that instead. He placed it behind his back with the butt above his belt. He took two magazines with seven rounds each, and slipped them into his pocket out of habit. He only needed one carefully placed round through the roof of his mouth into his brain. He knew he couldn't fuck that up. Brian grabbed the extra magazines just in case.

You never could tell just what the fuck might be waiting for you.

All that good Army training sure as fuck qualified me for something when I got back.

On the work bench lay a legal sized yellow pad and a pencil. Looking down at the pad he saw the list of materials he had once meant to buy to build a play house for Katie.

Meant to do a lot of things in this life...once.

He was home then, after his first tour, when the order came for a second tour. He hadn't caught his breath from the first tour. Dust covered the paper. Blowing it from the top sheet, he lovingly ran his fingers down the list of materials for an object he would never build for the daughter he would always love. Lying under the brilliant stars of the Afghan night sky he imagined cutting the planks and pounding the nails as he fashioned the playhouse for Katie.

Brian took the pencil and wrote a brief note to Barbara. He owed her that much.

It all led to this. The day he met her. Those summers in Speculator. The brief years of normality. The really good times they had had. Then the fucking ragheads had to go and screw everything up. The MREs with brown dust as a condiment served up to the stench of death. At home, a stranger without words. Over there, he'd been a soldier knowing he wouldn't go home in one piece. There was no longer so much as a spark of love. It was just home. The only guys who knew what the hell was going on were the guys over there.

But, he owed Barbara. He still felt something. It was like shouting over incoming artillery with his throat pouring out air and his lips framing words but no one hearing a sound. He felt obliged to leave some words for Barbara. The fingers of his right hand trembled in their embrace of the yellow pencil the way his arms once trembled when he held Barbara. Bringing the point of the pencil to just above the paper he hesitated before words fell from the pencil across the page. Not many, but enough. Satisfied, nodding, he dropped the pad onto the workbench causing a small puff of dust. Brian paused, reached inside the bag pulling out the bottle of Bourbon. He sipped the liquor.

He took another swig, admonishing himself not to get tanked up and drive off the road before he got where he needed to get to. He grinned at the thought of dying prematurely before he got to the place where he would kill himself.

Now that's fucking planning. Army fucking planning.

Brian walked from the house through the garage, leaving the door open. He climbed into the pickup, tossed the bag onto the seat next to him, and started the engine. As he backed the truck out of the driveway, he paused and looked back one last time at the house he had shared with Barbara, and eventually with Katie. Then, he abruptly forced the shift into reverse, and pressed his foot down hard against the accelerator. The tires spun against the cement driveway screeching and sending up a stream of dark smoke as the truck sped backwards to the road, and then swerved wildly on its path north.

CHAPTER 2

KATIE

THERE ONCE WAS A TIME TOGETHER

*B*arbara sat in front with a book. A wide straw hat shaded her face from the sun. Brian sat in the stern of the fifteen foot long green canoe guiding it toward lily pads on the far side of the lake. Brian cast one type of lure after another with no success. Either the bass weren't hitting that day or they simply weren't there.

Barbara looked over her shoulder at Brian. She smiled, mouthed, "I love you," and went back to her reading.

"They're not biting hon, I'm heading back to the dock. We can get some ice cream on the way home."

Barbara put her book down in her lap.

"No thanks. Remember our deal? I gave up the Haagen-Dazs and you're in a car pool. We're on our way, Brian to getting our first house."

They were a couple then. They talked, and shared, and loved. Now, she didn't know who Brian was, and she feared him. Barbara remembered how hard they saved money for a down payment on the ranch house. For an instant, Barbara saw Brian sitting at the dinette in the kitchen of their apartment with *a calculator and a legal sized pad calculating how many months it would take before they would have a down payment. Then, Barbara would sit on his lap, distract him, and they'd laugh in a loving embrace from the kitchen to the bedroom.*

And Katie. How much we both wanted Katie. How worried and protective Brian was all through the pregnancy. Finally, we got the money for the down payment, and made the offer and got the house. Brian worked all day at the dealership, did his drills, and at night, he worked on Katie's room. I remember coming down the hall, and watching him on his hands and knees sanding off layers of paint from the baseboard, just grinning, and laughing. Does any part of him even exist anymore?

Barbara stared at the young nurse as she exited the chilly office guiding little Katie in front of her. Perspiration beaded on Barbara's forehead and dampened her armpits despite the cool room. She wasn't sure whether the perspiration was from her dash across the parking lot with Katie in tow, and her haste up the stairs, or from anxiety as to what she would hear this morning. She opened her purse and removed a small packet of tissues. In doing so she noticed the small rectangular piece of plastic bag containing the wedding ring she no longer wore.

For a moment, her thoughts went to the ring. Did she really hope that somehow she and Brian would get back together? Like a sentry whose eyes slowly get heavy until he snaps the lids up, Barbara jerked herself alert. She looked around the waiting room to Dr. Han's office.

"You can go in and wait for the doctor," the receptionist said.

Barbara rose, opened the door between the waiting room and Doctor Han's office, and then sat uncomfortably in front of his cluttered desk. The desk was a living collage of periodicals, note pads, journals, and computer print outs. Barbara suddenly realized that Dr. Han had entered the room.

"I'm sorry," Dr. Han said. "I know how hard this is for you."

He paused, and then looked directly at Barbara. "Her liver function is continuing to decline. We've got to do whatever it takes to schedule the surgery."

Barbara jumped from her chair causing it to skid across the floor on round, flat pieces beneath its metal legs. She then turned away from Dr. Han who retained his impassive demeanor leaning back in his chair as if to give Barbara more space.

"I know! I know!"

She clasped her elbows with her palms. She looked over her shoulder at Dr. Han, and then away. Her back rose and fell as she took deep, excited breaths.

"It all depends on Mister McAfee."

Dr. Han hefted the manila folder in his right hand.

"There are no other options at this point. We need his cooperation."

Barbara turned, her eyes flashing with anger, and her arms shaking.

"That sonofabitch…."

Dr. Han raised his right arm as if he were a traffic cop. "Look, Barbara, whatever is going on between you and your husband…."

Dr. Han regretted the tone of his words as soon as he had spoken.

"Nothing is going on between me and Brian. It's over." She turned in a circle folding and unfolding her arms.

"He went off a soldier to that fucking war, again, and I don't know what they sent back to me this time."

She spun around facing Dr. Han. She raised her hands before her face pointing at Dr. Han.

"It took us a year the first time to get to where we could talk to each other like we knew each other! Can you imagine that? Send off a husband and get back some stranger? Can you?"

Dr. Han stepped back farther.

"He was a good man once. A good father. A husband." Barbara looked across the doctor's office and out the window as if looking into the past. "We had…those years…" She smiled faintly.

"And now…." Dr. Han said taking control of the conversation.

"It's none of my business, except for treating Katie. We're out of options except for Brian. The test results are clear. Katie suffers from a rare form of liver disease. Her liver is failing and she needs a transplant."

Dr. Han approached Barbara slowly, pointed to the chair, and she slumped in the chair.

Dr. Han leaned back against his desk.

"We," he smiled, "Katie doesn't have time to wait for a donor. We need a partial transplant from your husband."

Dr. Han's silence became the question.

Barbara did not respond.

"Assuming he's in good enough shape to do it. We need to examine him to see if he really is suitable."

"What about…can't we…can't I be the donor?"

"We've been through that Barbara. If you weren't pregnant…"

Dr. Han frowned.

"You still haven't told him have you?"

Dr. Han shook his head.

"You know, if you talk to him…"

"Talk to him!"

Barbara shouted, and then hearing the intensity of her scream put her hand to her mouth. When Brian had gotten home from the second tour they had made love and she had conceived. Shortly after that, their relationship dramatically changed for the worst.

Dr. Han stepped forward and placed his hands on Barbara's shoulders.

"Doctor, I didn't want him to know. Don't want him to know."

Barbara sobbed looking past Dr. Han, and then looked back at him.

"I don't know what he'd do."

Barbara's eyes pleaded.

"I don't know who he is anymore."

"He is the father," Dr. Han said.

"He hasn't been a father or a husband since he got back this last time."

"Has he talked to anyone?"

Dr. Han removed his glasses and rubbed his eyes with the thumb and forefinger of his right hand.

"Only himself and a whiskey bottle. He won't go to the VA anymore. He got tired of waiting for appointments, and when he did talk to someone they just wanted to write a script, dope him up, and get rid of him. He told me that going to the VA depressed him. He didn't find comfort in others having problems. So, he stopped trying. He just sits up all night and drinks until he passes out."

Barbara stared out of the window.

"How long has that been going on?"

Dr. Han took a ball point pen from his pocket, and prepared to write in the file.

"What?"

"How long has he been drinking heavily?"

"Two months, I guess."

Dr. Han frowned.

"You've got to get him to stop before he damages his liver."

Barbara rose again.

"I don't care; I wish he'd just get it over with."

Barbara rose, walked to the window and leaned against it trembling. Tears wet her face, dampened her hair and her breathing was deep.

"No. I didn't mean that."

Dr. Han walked to her placing his hands on her shoulders again. His palms pressed lightly against her.

Barbara laid her hands on his hands.

"We need him Barbara. You and Katie need him. We can take part of his healthy liver and transplant it to Katie. He's a perfect donor,

14

and her body's immune system will accept it. But, if he destroys it with alcohol...Barbara? Barbara?"

Turning back to Dr. Han, Barbara's eyes showed a steely resolve to confront Brian that evening, to do whatever it was that she had to do, to compel him to give up his self-destructive behavior to save Katie. Surely, thought Barbara Brian would respond to Katie even if he no longer did to her.

Dr. Han spoke into his intercom and ushered Barbara from his office into the waiting room. The door opened and the nurse brought in Katie.

"Let's go, Katie."

Barbara snatched her coat and Katie's from the coat rack, helped Katie put on her coat, and then turned, reaching for Katie's small hand. Grasping Katie's hand, Barbara quickly led the way from Dr. Han's office. Other patients in the hallway stepped aside as Barbara and Katie raced through them.

Barbara plucked her cell phone from her purse and called a close friend and the mother of one of Katie's friends. Barbara spoke rapidly, pleadingly, and then she closed the phone. She opened the door to the van, strapped Katie into her car seat, and then drove out of the hospital parking lot.

"Mommy?" Katie asked, "Aren't you driving too fast?"

Katie stared out of the window from her secure perch in a booster seat.

"You are, aren't you, Mommy?"

Barbara glanced down at the speedometer. She was doing fifty miles per hour in a thirty mile per hour zone.

"Yes, Katie, you're right. Mommy is going too fast. I'm sorry."

Barbara glanced at the speedometer, eased her foot on the gas pedal, and looked over her shoulder at Katie.

"Thanks, Katie."

"Okay, Mommy."

"Honey you're going to have a sleep over with Gracie, won't that be fun?"

"I like Gracie."

"I know you do, and Gracie's mommy is very nice."

Barbara paused, and looked in the rear view mirror at Katie strapped in her car seat.

"I need to talk with your daddy."

Katie looked out of the window at the houses and trees passing by as Barbara spoke. Without turning her gaze away from the window, Katie spoke.

"Daddy isn't happy."

"I know, honey."

"Does daddy love us anymore?"

Barbara slowed the van and parked it on the side of the street. She got out and walked around the van, opened the curbside door, and got in. She crouched in front of Katie, and put her hands on the little girl's shoulders. Barbara gently brushed Katie's long hair from her face.

"Your daddy loves you very, very much."

"Sometimes he has a sad face."

"Yes."

Barbara shook her head.

"Daddy is sad."

She took a deep breath. "Sometimes you get sad?"

"You cheer me up."

"I know, and we're trying with daddy. Katie, that's why you're going to Gracie's tonight. So your mommy can try to cheer up Daddy."

"Will that make it better?"

Barbara fussed over Katie's blouse and jacket, kissed her on the forehead, and then paused by the open door to the van.

"I hope so, honey."

CHAPTER 3

THE ROAD NORTH

To Honor A Fallen Comrade

*B*rian *stepped quietly through the outpost, made his way to the wire, and dropped his trousers. He stared up at the brilliant stars in the clear Afghan night sky against the backdrop of encircling mountain ridges. He shivered slightly releasing an arcing, steaming spray of urine into the air raining down on the parched Afghan soil. He felt great satisfaction in pissing on the soil of these ungrateful, miserable bastards he was defending. A few meters away he saw teeth sparkle in moonlight. Swiveling his M4 carbine up, he fired. The rounds struck home across the chest of the lone Taliban.*

Behind Brian, spot lights flashed on. The thud of mortar rounds fired from within the outpost came, and then the pop above of illumination shells arcing down in a slow pendulum swing suspended from small parachutes.

"What you got, Mac?" First Sergeant Howard Walker shouted.

An EOD specialist bent down carefully cutting the dead Talban's garments with surgical scissors. Beneath the robes was the blood soaked harness of plastic explosives, and a single button detonator attached to the end of an electric cord.

"Sombitch, Mac, that's another decoration for you. Stopping a suicide bomber. What's that make, Mac? Three? Four? You got four Bronze Stars, Mac? Audie fucking Murphy McAfee. I'll tell you, Mac, you can stand near me in the chow line or in the field any time you want to. Three rounds into this mother and not one of them hit the explosives? You are definitely tap dancing in the shadow of death, son. You are one fine soldier, son. Sam is lucky to have you. I am lucky to have you. Your wife and child are lucky to have you."

Brian pressed the button on the arm rest causing the driver's side window to roll down. The rush of cool air across his fevered brow soothed him. Eschewing the Northway, he drove up Route 38 away from Amsterdam and into the Adirondacks. There was little traffic other than the locals as he drove north. Reaching inside his shirt pocket he took out the carefully folded letter he had received from Henry Two Pines. A smile appeared and then vanished from his face.

Henry Two Pines had been a surrogate father to Johnnie True Blood, and Brian had met them both where he had spent summers in Speculator at a camp with Johnnie True Blood. Lessons in life, racism, the "haves" versus the "have-nots" passed from the older man to the young ones without them feeling that they were being taught. Henry Two Pines was one of the few adults Brian and Johnnie True Blood enjoyed spending time with.

It seemed to the two of them that Henry Two Pines knew just about everything that was important to know. Over the summers they spent together the two youngsters learned many things from Henry Two Pines. Whether he was teaching them to navigate without a compass, or to make a fire without matches, or to find food in the wilderness, there was a moral to the tale they discovered after they mastered the craft at hand. Each them discovered that later when faced with challenges and cross roads at key points in their lives. Each of them felt that they could almost look over their shoulder and see Henry Two Pines nodding his approval at what they had just chosen to do.

The letter was a last link between Brian and Johnnie True Blood. Holding the letter, Brian heard "Taps" playing softly in the background. Brian thought of Henry Two Pines burying Johnnie True Blood on Indian land in the custom of his people. *How the hell did the old man swing that?* Brian shook his head and stuck the envelope back in his pocket.

Coming to see you, Johnnie. Pay my respects. And then...

Brian's right foot pressed down against the accelerator. His fingers clutched hard against the vibrating wheel of the speeding truck. He glanced from the speedometer to the road ahead and back. He passed the legal speed limit for the un-posted section of state highway and sped upward into the range of reckless driving. Taking curves too fast he felt the rear end of the truck fight to keep traction and not spin around. His heart pounded. Reaching down he punched the scan buttons of the radio until loud, pounding rock music filled the cab of the pickup truck. He sped past partly functioning farms, and ramshackle farm stands. He drove past garages with dozens of deer antlers nailed over the door. He drove past nearly abandoned farms where farm equipment had been left in the fields, and boarded up gas stations bereft of customers. Long, drab shadows fell across the countryside. The stark, simple contrast of black and white suited him at that moment.

Several times oncoming motorists glared at his driving as they passed him by. He didn't trouble himself with their disapproval. The farther north Brian traveled the fewer cars he encountered. North of Great Sacandaga Lake the road began its slow, steady ascent into the thickly forested rolling hills. The woods came down to the shoulders of the narrow highway.

At one point in his journey north the strip of heavily patched asphalt curved and twisted along the side of ridges overlooking rushing white water in streams far below. Trout were safe in these streams at the foot of a sheer precipice which few fishermen chose to descend. As he drove through towns like Wells, past the general store on the west side of the road, and made the curve past the now deserted public beach he noticed general stores where he and Barbara had purchased firewood or supplies on one of their many camping trips.

He smiled thinking back to those innocent, illicit pleasures and how sweet life was then. How simple it was?

Money for gas. Money for beer and condoms. A couple of days in a sleeping bag in the woods. That was life.

The trip north was a parallel passage through time to the place where he had known the happiest moments in his life. This only deepened his sadness. It had all begun there especially his boyhood with Johnnie True Blood. The two played Cowboys and Indians with the Indians winning more often than the Cowboys. They played soldier. Each perfected his own dying last moments complete with dramatic fall and last words.

His love for Barbara began up there. In that general store they'd been under age and paid a college student to buy beer for them. Brian remembered the way the "older man" had looked at Barbara, how that stranger's envy of Brian had filled him with masculine pride. That drugstore where Brian first bought a package of condoms instead of using those handed down from the elders among the camp counselors; the college students in their early twenties. He remembered discarding the condom that he had carried in his wallet so long that the aluminum foil wrapping had worn through.

Mile after mile of thick woods passed by as Brian sped north up the narrow, two lane asphalt road. Suddenly, the woods surrendered territory to the gravel parking lot of the Tamarack Lodge.

This place called to Brian. He stopped the pickup in the parking lot before the log cabin restaurant and bar. The parking lot was as square as a parade ground. The single story building had green shutters.

He smiled as he saw them all en masse at first. The whole pale gray group loitered in the parking lot. Brian made out the old ones. Revolution. Eighteen Twelve. Mexican-American. Civil War. Spanish

American. World War I. World War II. Korea. Vietnam. Gulf. Iraq. Afghanistan.

This unrecognized corner of the Adirondacks sent its youth to every conflict. Brian rendered a quick salute to the spirit image soul of a twenty five year old volunteer who died at Andersonville looking sixty. Their eyes met. Brian held his salute, the trooper returned it, and then Brian pulled back onto the road and continued his passage north. That parcel of woods faded from sight.

Unseen by Brian, men in the photographs on the wall of the Tamarack lodge jumped out of 1940 Ford convertibles, Chevys' with tail fins in the fifties, pickup trucks, and sauntered as the young immortals do, across the gravel parking lot with the other translucent shapes.

Tamarack Lodge. Brian smiled weakly. When he and Barbara were seventeen they sat at the end of the bar in the Tamarack Lodge and sipped gin and tonics. Being under-age in Pete's didn't matter much then if you behaved yourself.

The sun touched down upon the tops of the tall trees to the west of the road causing wide, black shadow to cross Brian's path. He turned down the volume on the radio and slowed the truck. He was close now.

He arrived at Lake Pleasant patting the small green canvas bag on the seat next to him containing the Colt .45 automatic pistol.

So many years before, it had been so different here. He caught sight of the lake off to his left. The wind tossed surface of the lake shimmered sending silver waves rolling thoughts and dreams across its surface to him. He loved this place. He always had. His throat constricted as he looked through the windshield of the truck at the lake. Through the open window, he heard the soothing slap of the waves against the brown sand of the public beach.

He slowed the truck looking up the beach to a narrow strip of sand at the edge of the woods. The memory was so fresh in his mind he thought for an instant he might even be able to make out the foot prints that he and Barbara had left in the sand so many years before. Suddenly, he stopped the truck, and pulled into the parking lot. Stepping down from the truck he walked across the recently paved asphalt parking lot onto the beach.

So many years before.

He looked up around the lake at the surrounding woods.

How could all that happened since then have happened? Couldn't I just somehow turn the clock back and undo it? Could I go back and make a different choice in time and somehow end up in a different place than I am?

In his mind's eye he saw that day, he and Barbara beneath a dented, scratched aluminum canoe. There had been a light rain, the rain tapping on the canoe's metal skin, keeping others away from the beach. He popped his head out from under the canoe looking across the public beach to keep them from being discovered as they made love. He heard her voice from years before as he stared at the spot where the canoe had been. Her voice from the past was clearer now than her voice in the present. They loved the Adirondacks and vowed that they would go off and have careers, get married, and then return here to a simple life of loving each other.

Barbara wore a two piece, green floral print bathing suit contrasting seductively to her deep tan, and he had on a pair of red trunks with a Red Cross Water Safety Instructor patch. Barbara waited tables at the old inn, and Brian was a camp counselor and waterfront director at a summer camp. He only had one night off a week, and he spent it with Barbara. Instantly after an evening together with her his thoughts were on the next night they would be together. In those days, they counted the hours they were apart.

He felt overwhelming darkness and sadness. His lips trembled. He forced his thumb and forefinger against his teeth to stifle his cry. He shook his head, got back in the truck, and drove slowly on through the town. Soon, he was north of town. He saw the old sign stained by rain and made a right turn off the asphalt road. The truck bounced going from the asphalt to the dirt track. The forest on both sides of the narrow dirt road was thick and grew over the top of the road. At the end of the narrow track Brian parked the truck before Henry Two Pines' trailer.

The trailer was an ancient old single-wide mounted on four neat stacks of gray cement blocks. The faded metal trim on its exterior was warped, cracked, and peeling away from the body. Vines nestled in the cracks, their tendrils grasping the metal skin. Dust had become dirt, and the dirt had accepted seeds, the seeds becoming vines. A thick layer of damp pine needles lay on top of the trailer obscuring the metal roof and making the trailer almost appear a natural part of the forest. A faintly discernible hue of what appeared to be yellow was the legacy of the original color. Atop the trailer a bent and mangled television antenna shared roof space with a new dish. Over the years, it had sustained uncountable dings and dents from falling pine cones, and pale, dry, pine limbs knocked from the trunks of overhanging pines by strong winds, and heavy wet snow.

Behind the trailer was a neatly tended small corral and barn. Angie, a chestnut mare, stepped from the barn into the corral at the sound of Brian's approach. Brian parked the truck, leaned against the steering wheel, and took a deep breath. The thin aluminum door opened and Henry Two Pines stepped down. He peered at the windshield of the truck, and then recognizing Brian walked quickly to it. Brian opened the door and got out. The two men embraced.

"Brian, Brian," Henry Two Pines said.

Behind them, Angie neighed and slapped her hooves on the earth in her corral.

"Henry."

Henry stepped back and slapped Brian on both shoulders. "You look…"

Henry stopped in mid sentence seeing the look in Brian's eyes, the deep pockets under his eyes, and the lines on his forehead. Looking down he saw the younger man's right hand tremble slightly.

Angie trotted back and forth in her corral. Henry looked over his shoulder at her.

"I think she remembers you."

Brian reached back inside the truck and grabbed his bag. A bottle of Bourbon fell out on the soft earth. Henry Two Pines watched as Brian bent down, picked it up, and put it back in his bag. The older man noticed the .45 automatic in the bag. His eyes met Brian's but no words were exchanged.

"C'mon."

Henry Two Pines gestured toward the trailer. He held the door for Brian who went up the stairs, entered the living room and sat on the couch. Henry sat nearby in the easy chair. Folding his hands in his lap, Henry waited. Brian looked away, and then back at Henry.

"I came to pay my respects to him."

"He would like that."

Henry nodded toward the west.

"His body is with the others. His soul…."

Henry smiled and nodded.

Brian reached inside the bag for the bottle. As he began to uncap it, Henry Two Pines rose, went to the kitchen, opened a cabinet, and returned with a plastic glass.

"Here," he said handing the glass to Brian.

Brian poured a few inches of Bourbon into the glass. He nodded at the glass, and then at Henry. Henry shook his head.

"You look awful. You haven't been good to yourself."

"Yeah, I know. He's with the others?"

"Where you two used to hunt."

Brian nodded. He took a long swallow. It was still inside the trailer. Time seemed to be slowing down. Brian listened to the gentle wind outside, and to the ticking clock atop the refrigerator. He felt the slow steady beat of his heart.

"I remember."

Brian took another drink.

"You hungry? I can rustle up something?"

"Maybe later."

"You going in the morning?"

Brian thought long about Henry's question, and then answered.

"Yes, Henry, I'm going in the morning."

He refilled the plastic cup. Placing the bottle on the low coffee table in front of him, Brian fell back on the couch fast asleep. Henry Two Pines took a folded blanket from the side of the couch, unfolded it, and covered Brian with it as if he were draping a flag over a coffin. Henry knew why Brian had come.

In the morning Brian awoke to the smell of coffee and the scent of pancakes. Falling from the couch to the floor, Brian jumped to his feet, and ran down the steps of the trailer. Slamming the door open, he ran to the edge of the woods, bent over with his hands on his knees, and vomited. His body shook violently as his stomach purged itself. Finally, he was able to stand up. He walked back into the trailer, noticed his green bag on the kitchen table, and the .45 next to it. Slipping the .45 back into the bag, he poured himself a cup of coffee, and stepped outside. He took a sip of the coffee, instantly felt queasy, and vomited again. Bent over in front of the trailer, he heard Henry Tall Pines and Angie approach.

"You well enough to ride?"

Henry Two Pines frowned.

"You don't look well enough to walk."

Brian shook his head.

"Angie knows the way. She'll take you."

Henry paused.

"She'll find her way back, too."

Henry Two Pines stared into Brian's eyes.

Brian went back into the trailer and came back outside carrying the green bag. He slipped the strap over his shoulder.

"Henry," Brian said.

"Are you sure? At least I got to ask you that."

"Yes," Brian said softly.

Henry Two Pines embraced Brian.

"I could try to stop you."

"You couldn't. Let's not end our friendship like that."

Brian's eyes glistened with tears.

"Besides, before long I'll be with Johnnie. A better place."

"A better place," responded Henry Two Pines.

Brian put his left foot into the stirrup, grasped the horn with his left hand, and then pulled himself into the saddle. Angie stepped back, looked to Henry Two Pines who nodded, and stroked her forehead. Henry Two Pines stepped aside as Angie started down the trail through the thick forest to Johnnie True Blood's grave site.

CHAPTER 4
DRESS REHEARSAL
NO COMFORT IN SHARED GUILT

Young Brian leaned back in the shadow of a tall oak shading the corral of Henry Two Pines. Single streaks of black grease adorned his cheeks. His long hair was tucked up under a gray cowboy hat. His chest rose and fell rapidly as he tried to control his breathing and not reveal himself to his foe.

Johnnie True Blood moving stealthily between shadows surrounding the barn crept closer to his enemy. He was bare-chested with his long hair restrained by a camouflage head band. He crouched low and remained still. Cloaked by stillness in the shadow he was almost invisible. Resting his hand on the soft earth he felt the imprint of Brian's sneaker. Johnnie True Blood smiled, tossed a dried pine limb to his right, and then dashed to his left around the corral.

Brian turned to his left, raised his toy rifle, and awaited the appearance of his foe. Feeling the breath of his friend on his neck, Brian dropped his rifle, laughed, and turned to face his him.

"You've got to get up pretty early in the morning to fool me," Johnnie True Blood said laughing.

"Yeah, you got me," Brian said patting Johnnie True Blood on the shoulder. They turned away from the corral and walked slowly toward Henry Two Pines' trailer.

"You know what I been thinking?" Johnnie True Blood asked.

"No," said Brian. "What."

"I been thinking I'm gonna' be a soldier. A few more years I can enlist."

"Really? Guys gettin' blown up pretty good in Iraq." Johnnie True Blood smiled.

"That's where the war is. We could go together. Buddies."

"Yeah," Brian said putting his arm around Johnnie True Blood's shoulder. "Buddies."

"Hey, who's that girl you got the letter from today?"

"She's no girl, that's Barbara. Just a friend of mine."

Sitting in her driveway, slumped behind the steering wheel of her car, tears smearing her makeup, Barbara knew she had to get Brian to do what Katie needed him to do. Barbara's hands still cradling the steering wheel, she laid her head on her hands and sobbed. Tears fell across the narrow band of white skin on her ring finger where her wedding ring used to be. Unconsciously, she rubbed her ring finger with her left hand.

Away from Katie, Barbara was able to drop the façade of strength she maintained for her daughter. Barbara would get through all of this, but God knows she had no idea why it was being visited upon her.

Barbara looked skyward as if some answer were resident in the empty gray clouds above her head. She stared into the clouds as if waiting for a visage to form confirming her faith. She had adhered to the tenets of her church upbringing, had followed the Golden Rule, had always been faithful to Brian, and paid unto Caesar what was his due. Didn't that count for something? So many other people went their own way and did better in this life.

No. Don't go there. It isn't you. Deal with what you're dealt. Take care of Katie.

Seeing that the garage door was left open, another sign of Brian's irresponsibility, she was momentarily annoyed, felt her heart beat rise, and then waving her hand before her chest, let the moment pass. She had to. She took a deep breath.

"No.

Barbara waved her finger at the garage door.

"You're not going to get me going. I've got to focus. For Katie."

Grateful that Brian was not home, no doubt if he had been it would have led to an argument, she got out of the car, and walked up the flagstone path to the front door. She shook her head looking down at the path and then to the dark house. It wasn't that many years ago that this house had been so important to her and to Brian. She stumbled. Her shoe heel cracked against a loose stone that Brian had meant to fix for more than a year. She barely caught herself before striking the ground. She stared down at the loose stone.

"Damn it, Brian, I don't care how depressed you are! I can't take it anymore! You have to snap out of it! You have to get over it!"

Startled by her shouts, Barbara clasped her left hand over her mouth, looked up and down the street grateful that no one was watching her, and walked quickly to the front door. Fumbling for the key she looked to the open garage door, thought of closing it, and then dismissed the idea. Unlocking the door, and then stepping inside the dark house, she closed the door with a push of her shoulder, and leaned back against it. There was a stale smell to this house. There really wasn't much point to doing more than keeping it swept. Reaching, without looking, for the light switch she turned on the wall lamp in the living room. Across the cardboard boxes in the room she saw into the dining room.

The heavy oak dining room table now rested oddly on three legs. She remembered the percussion of the moment when the fourth leg had been jarred loose under the force of Brian's right fist slamming down atop the table. It was his first night home at the end of his second tour.

Barbara and Katie had waited for him at the airport until three in the morning. His plane had been delayed by bad weather. More asleep than awake, Katie had greeted her father and then fallen asleep in his arms on the drive on the way home. Later, after Barbara had tucked Katie in she found Brian waiting impatiently in the dining room. Brian embraced Barbara, kissed her on the neck and guided her toward their bedroom.

"No," Barbara had said softly. "I'm too tired; I'm going to sleep with Katie tonight."

Without a second of hesitation Brian turned away and slammed his fist down on the dining room table with a force resulting in a cannon crack of sound. Barbara jumped back terrified by Brian's act, ran to her bedroom, shut the door behind her, and locked it.

Barbara stepped softly into the dining room as if she were an intruder. There, on the wall, the dark background of an oil portrait with a gilt frame around a benign spinster dressed in white looked back at her. Barbara smiled. She found the painting at a yard sale, and adopted the image as some long distant family member. She hadn't paid very much for it, though she felt guilty for spending the few dollars that she had. She convinced herself that with Brian in Afghanistan he would come home and assume the painting had always been there. The woman in the painting looked to Barbara as if she were some long lost unknown relative. Aunt Alma had become her confidante, and on more than one night, Barbara had taken a bottle of gin, a bottle of ginger ale, and sat by herself at the table confiding in Aunt Alma. She did this a lot during Brian's first tour when his e-mails frightened her.

At first, the e-mails were driven by loneliness. Then, the e-mails became a litany of mundane existence. They described traffic on Barbara's way to work; how bad the food was when Brian and his platoon were back in the Forward Operating Base. And then, the e-mails from Brian changed. Where in the beginning of his tour he had never indicated exactly what he was doing, he now described in hideous detail what he saw; the bodies, the wounded, the sights and sounds. And, then, the e-mails stopped all together.

Brian and Barbara tried but quickly stopped using streaming video. Neither was particularly good at concealing emotions and their live audio and video simply made each of them feel worse. He would cite one item after another on a list of things he wanted her to do, and she would offer one excuse after another as to why she hadn't done them.

Slipping her shoes from her feet she made her way to the kitchen, reached up into a cabinet above the sink and found the square, frosted bottle of gin, and then took a bottle of ginger ale from the refrigerator. Dropping a few ice cubes into a high ball glass she poured in several ounces of gin, and then covered it with ginger ale. Returning to the dimly lit dining room, she sat on a cardboard box, raised her glass in a toast to Aunt Alma, and took a sip.

"Now what, Aunt Alma?"

Barbara looked at her watch.

"Any minute he ought to be here. Here, not home."

Leaning back against the wall she lifted her legs atop a cardboard box.

Heartwarming and disheartening images from the past competed for her attention. She saw the grin on Brian's face after they'd made love the first time beneath that canoe in Speculator. She clung to the good memories of Brian in the hope that he would somehow return to her, and they could reclaim their life together. At times she thought there was some fundamental failing within her which forced Brian from her.

Barbara took a long sip of the gin and ginger ale no longer feeling bitterness. Bitterness had become fatigue; and she had never been chronically more fatigued than she was now. The smallest of activities were a challenge. Her daily routine and striving to function were a challenge. No matter how many times Barbara thought through all the events and conversations leading up to Brian's decision to join the National Guard, it always came out the same no matter how many different ways she imagined she could have said something, or done something, to stop him. It wasn't supposed to have worked out like this. This wasn't the plan that Brian and Barbara had.

She was angry. Others had not gone. She looked out of the dining room across the dark living room as if she could see through the walls of the house and accuse with her eyes all who were more than content for those who chose to serve to serve in their places. She remembered reading of citizens in the Civil War who paid others to serve for them. Now, the few who had chosen to serve while the rest of the country looked the other way, and only a handful of soldiers and their families, bore the burdens and made the sacrifices while the majority of their countrymen ignored them and went about living their own lives in peace.

What had been lacking about her that would even let Brian make such a choice? How could Brian leave her and the love she had for him to go to war? How could a father leave his daughter? Had she been something more, somehow, would he have stayed and their life together unaltered by the demon touch of war? What was wrong with her? Was her shortcoming the reason her marriage and daughter were in peril?

She finished her drink, rose, and walked to the kitchen. She added ginger ale to the gin in the glass, swirled it around in her hand, and then took a long sip.

Looking at the watch on her wrist she noticed that it was late, even for Brian screwing up another job interview and stopping off somewhere for too many beers to safely drive home. He should have been home by now. Funny she thought, she used to dread his arrival home, and the inevitable arguments which ensued, or the silence as they each sought separate quarters, and now she was anxious for his return. She needed him home this night.

She walked through the kitchen, and opened the door to the garage. His truck was still not back. Noticing the open door to the wall locker, the padlock hanging from the bracket, and knowing what he kept there, she flashed.

"You stupid sonofabitch, how could you leave that open with a child in the house, and the garage door open?"

Walking quickly to the wall locker she removed the padlock from the clasp and slammed the door shut. She saw the open tackle box on the work bench instantly noting what was missing. A yellow pad was on the workbench. Placing her drink on the dusty wood surface she lifted the pad. The top page, the one with the list of materials was flipped back.

She read. Her eyes darted across the words ahead of her thoughts and her fears.

"Dear Barbara," began the note as Barbara read slowly.

"I let you down. We never did build that cabin. Dreams we never made happen. Only one way out for all of us. I read the fine print in the insurance policy. You and Katie will have money. It's been long enough. 'No defense against suicide.' Brian."

Barbara clutched the note to her chest.

"Oh my god!"

CHAPTER 5

SOULS STIR

NO HIGHER PURPOSE

"*G*reat spirit, we give you the soul of Johnnie True Blood. My heart is heavy with sorrow. The tribe forever laments his passing so young. He was a good man. A good son who truly loved and honored his mother. He was a strong warrior of brave heart and fierce courage."*

Henry Two Pines reached into his pouch and removed several small objects.

"Bronze Star for valor before the enemy."

He took the second object.

"Soldier's Medal for saving the life of his comrades."

Henry Two Pines held the medals in the palms of his hands raising and lowering them as if scales assessing their weight, and then placed them atop the blanket covering Johnnie True Blood's chest.

Henry Two Pines gently covered the body with soft earth, and then took a deep breath and wailed. The first notes rose in a sharp tonal progression. Ensuing notes followed in a step ladder of wails from the earth to the sky in the path of the soul on its course to the spirit world. The wails of the shaman grew louder and echoed from the clearing through the nearby valleys. Reaching down for a small cage, he opened the door releasing a bird which swiftly flew into the now bright blue sky and disappeared.

Henry slowly turned in a circle, nodded to the earth, and nodded to the sky. Gently, he took Angie's reins, and then walked in the lead with Angie trailing close behind him. When he paused and his shoulders hunched as he let out a low cry, Angie softly nuzzled him between the shoulders gently pushing him toward the barn and home.

Struggling like a drowning man under water in sight of light above, Johnnie True Blood clawed with his hands, pulled with his arms, and kicked with his legs. With all of his power he forced and willed himself toward the light.

No longer was Johnnie True Blood immersed in cold, shrouded in darkness, and enveloped in the stale sweet smell of death and the dust of ages. What had seemed like a brief moment of darkness was no more. No longer was there unbearable pain nor a depth of blackness in a wandering, spiral descent. No longer was darkness enveloping his heart and soul.

Awareness came to Johnnie True Blood. There was light here; a buoyant levitating light within the stillness. It was so still that Johnnie True Blood listened to the blood coursing through the arteries of his brain down to the capillaries. The bright white light surrounding him vibrated as if a living entity. He was not frightened. The light seemed to call to him in a calming though unspoken voice. He realized his eyes were open, he was whole, and he was in the present.

A fire was before him in the center of the small clearing atop a forested hill. The fire burned without consuming the flame cradled wood. Red and yellow ribbons of flame spun around and through the stack of wood. An offering of gray smoke rose skyward as if from a long tobacco pipe passed among unseen elders. He felt a sense of others from long ago around him though he could not see them. It was good to be in this place. Henry Two Pines had told the young

Johnnie True Blood stories of this place. Johnnie looked down from the slope at the gently curving slope below.

His senses were vibrantly alive. Memories from a different time crouched like unseen beasts deep within a dark cave where men feared to tread. He couldn't see them, but he knew they were there. Somehow, this fire seemed to keep those memories at bay protecting him.

How did he get here? Where had he been? Is this real? Was he alive? Was it only this day when the Taliban killed him?

He leaned back against the moss covered trunk of an ancient oak, and slowly slid down to the earth. On the back side of the oak, nearly seven feet off the ground were the recent claw marks of a brown bear. Several inches under the bark was an Iroquois arrowhead from hundreds of years ago grown over by the living tree.

For that moment he felt as if he had always been in this place, against this tree, with this fire before him. There was no moment before or after this one; only this moment. His left hand reached out and down and touched a bulging part of the trunk before its mass slipped beneath the cold soil. He could almost feel the life within the wood.

His vision clearer now, he saw that he was on a white, folded wool blanket with broad blue and red parallel stripes. Reaching out he picked up a can of corned beef with a red and white label. He looked down at the can of corn, pack of Lucky Strikes, and pint bottle of whiskey. The fingers of his right hand slipped beneath the Bronze Star and Soldiers Medal lifting them. He felt the memories contained within each. He saw around the globe to a place and time which were no more. He raised the can of corned beef in his left hand as if it was a glass and he was making a toast.

"Henry Two Pines," he said softly.

The wind snatched his words from his lips and carried them across the sky.

"You sweet old man. I love you, old man."

Johnnie True Blood sat cross-legged on the blanket before the crackling, aromatic campfire. Looking from within the closely nestled pines, surrounding him like a cohort of former comrades, his eyes surveyed the tops of nearby mountains.

The blanket beneath him was new and identical to one his father had given his mother many years before. Johnnie True Blood felt the virgin pile of the coarse wool with his finger tips. A torrent of pleasant memories from the good times in his childhood flickered across his mind's eye. The tactile sensation sent tingling electric shocks up his arm. He remembered playing on the blanket as a very young child. He could smell the fragrant scent of pancakes frying on the wood stove by his mother and savored the taste of maple syrup. That was the time, so very brief, when he had known a family of father and mother. His mother died young from breast cancer, and his father died young from drunkenly driving his pickup into a tree the day of his mother's funeral.

He smiled broadly. Opening his arms, turning his hands palms up toward the sky, he gently bowed his head in profound reverence for this moment. He breathed in deeply air as fresh and clean as if he were the first person to ever breathe it. It was as if creation began this day with him. The air filled his lungs with a sweet taste, and made his head giddy. He looked at his hands and arms, and then grasped his right wrist with his left hand, and his left wrist with his right hand. It seemed that he was real again. He seemed to be touching flesh and the bone within. He shook his head and laughed softly. What did it matter? This was all beyond his understanding. There was a peace and a pleasure to it. Why question? His laughter grew louder, and louder still. Soon, the tones of his laughter echoed across the valley.

His soul reveled in the sheer ecstasy of his human senses. The abrupt absence of constant pain in his life would have been joy enough for him, but this moment he was in paradise. He grinned for a moment at the thought of whether the mujahedeen might be here as well, gathered around an oasis in the forest awaiting their reward of virgins. All paths lead to one place? He looked across the clearing and to the forested ridges surrounding him.

Like regaining one's senses after a firefight, he remembered. He had been someone, somewhere, and then it all changed and he was someone different, someplace else, and then it was over, and he was back. Back where? He was surely himself this moment with all of his memories intact.

Stretching his arms wide, there was a peace in his heart which he had never known, and the depth of it so overwhelmed him that he chose to no longer question it.

Let the faith that resides within abide.

He looked skyward. Your purpose, he thought. He took a deep breath reveling in the sensation.

Robust flickering reddish arms of fire welcomed him; the yellow firelight reflecting in his eyes, the snap and hiss of the fire singing to him, and he listening carefully for the words hidden within the fire's song. He knew it spoke to him; he had only to be patient to understand the words. Henry Two Pines had spoken of this time to him. He knew at that moment that he was one with all around, below, and above him. There was a unity in his soul and spirit.

Then, he understood the words from the fire. What he heard was great and true. He nodded and smiled grinning broadly. Reaching up he touched his face, warm with the heat of the fire, while the bare back of his neck was cooled by the night wind. His front bathed in light; the setting sun cloaked his back in darkness.

Silver white tree limbs, some clattering together like the horns of rutting bucks, swayed and rattled in the wind. A full moon appeared pushing dark gray clouds apart to present itself to Johnnie True Blood, suddenly casting the clearing in the valley below in a brilliant silver hue reflecting the moonlight back to the night sky.

"Brian," Johnnie True Blood said.

He gazed down once more at his hands and smiled knowing his purpose. He rose, raised his arms over his head, drew in the fullness of breath he could hold, and shouted the name of his friend to the four corners.

Then, Johnnie True Blood heard it. He cocked his head listening. A voice in the wind called out his own name to him. Brian's words seemed to take shape in the air before him. And then, Johnnie True Blood saw the face of his friend.

"Come my friend, come quickly," Johnnie True Blood said softly.

CHAPTER 6
SHOOTING GALLERY
SUSPENSION OF TIME

Part One of Parable: WHY DID YOU GO?

S*ergeants Brian McAfee and Johnnie True Blood ran through smoke, dust, and gunfire. Brian's throat was dry. He tried shouting over the thunder of explosions and small arms fire to no avail. Behind them gunners atop the HUM-V's walked fifty caliber fire across mud walls, boulders, and other likely hiding places for those who had just triggered the IED.*

The green lieutenant the two sergeants had picked up moments before at the battalion headquarters sat frozen in the HUM-V. His words of winning the war single handedly were forgotten.

Villagers crouched behind mud walls in fear of their lives from the Taliban and the Americans. The Taliban responsible for the IED huddled within the groups of innocent townspeople. Nearing the Toyota HiAce bus, called a "falang" by the locals, Brian saw that the metal body of the bus opened like a flower bursting into bloom with metal shard petals wet with fresh, red blood. Arms, hands, fingers, eyes, indiscernible chunks of flesh and bone, some still quivering, radiated out from the smoldering bus.

Quickly, Brian and Johnnie True Blood crawled among the dead and dying seeking any to save. The two soldiers were soon drenched in the blood of the victims of the Taliban IED. Brian and Johnnie didn't notice that their comrades had ceased firing.

The perpetrators now stood in the gathering mob gesturing angrily at the Americans and urging on other protesters. Villagers surrounded Brian and Johnnie True Blood. Back to back, Brian and Johnnie faced the angry villagers shouting and taunting at them. The men pointed at the American soldiers in blood stained uniforms. Brian did not need a translator to understand their hostility. Brian nodded at Johnnie True Blood who nodded back at him. Noticing a mangled goat writhing in agony on the road Brian took his .45 automatic from its holster, and walked toward the dying animal. Before he got there, a villager bent low, and with one stroke of a sharp Choora slit the goat's throat. Glaring at Brian, the villager lifted the goat and carried it into the village dripping blood behind him as he walked.

"Welcome to the war," Johnnie True Blood said.

He patted Brian on the shoulder and gestured toward the newly arrived lieutenant, a distinguished military graduate from ROTC, who vomited at the side of the road.

Angie trotted from the trail in the woods into the clearing and stopped bathed in the light of the full moon. Tossing her mane, she chortled, waited for Brian to notice, and then tossed her mane again. Brian patted Angie on the neck. His fingers lingered in her mane.

He stared at the slight earthen dome of the burial mound silhouetted by the moonlight against the slope. The lighter color of the fresh grave dug by Henry Two Pines was apparent even in the reflected light. Momentarily confused, Brian looked up the hill, and then dismounted with his green bag in his hand. He stood next to Angie for a moment, and then he gently patted Angie on her hind quarter. Angie swiftly turned, and trotted back up the trail toward home.

"Thanks, girl," Brian said.

He watched Angie disappear around the bend in the trail. He suddenly sobered up from the excess of the night before. He felt very alone standing in this clearing deep in the woods at night. Swinging the bag in his right hand he walked across the clearing toward the grave.

He wondered how many others had been interred there as his eyes scanned the girth of the mound. Finding Johnnie True Blood's grave where Henry had said it would be, Brian stood still, and then knelt. Overwhelmed by grief he collapsed. His fingers clenched earth as his tears dampened it.

"Johnnie...Johnnie..."

Brian rose slowly. Something was wrong. This was the place, but it wasn't. He turned in a circle eyeing the surrounding hills.

"You sombitch," Brian said.

He grinned.

Turning away from the grave containing the corpse of Johnnie True Blood, slipping his pack over his shoulder, Brian ascended the steep slope to the east in search of his friend. The combination of starlight and moonlight was enough for him to see as he ascended along an old game trail. For more than an hour he pulled himself up the slope by grasping tree branches and the narrow trunks of small trees. Rocks kicked loose by his passage tumbled down. He reached a clearing atop the knoll surrounded by a stand of hardwood trees. Hunched over he gasped for breath from his exertion.

"That's it."

Brian saw the yellowish white light from the fire. He caught the scent of it as he surveyed the small clearing in the distance as if he were point man to a squad of infantry looking for mines and IED.

Slowly, he stepped forward passing through and around tree trunks. Now, he heard the crackling of a fire. Stepping from darkness into light Brian stared into the fire realizing that there was no ash, and that that the logs seemed not to burn though surrounded in flames. The heat quickly dried his sweat soaked clothes. He reached into his pack, brought the bottle to his lips and swallowed, welcoming the reassuring touch of the burning liquid down his throat. He dropped the pack to his feet as he drank while slowly turning around to scan the clearing around the fire. His eyes met those of Johnnie True Blood.

Brian recoiled at the sight of his dead friend. Brian jumped back away from Johnnie True Blood instinctively reacting to danger. Fear soon dissolved into wonder. Brian stopped.

"No fear, Mac. I been waiting."

"You knew I was coming?"

"Yes," Johnnie True Blood said.

"Where are we?"

Johnnie True Blood laughed.

"You are in the woods north of Speculator. What you really mean is where am I?"

Brian nodded.

"Why am I not afraid of you?"

He glanced at the fire.

"Of this?"

"Why should you be? You knew me most of my life."

"You're dead, Johnnie!"

Brian looked at the bottle of whiskey. Maybe he was in the tertiary stage of alcoholism and this was a hallucination.

Johnnie True Blood looked down at the backs and palms of his seemingly opaque hands.

"It feels good. Never felt better. Feel like I've always been here. God, what a moon. Ain't that beautiful tonight?"

Brian turned away from Johnnie True Blood and then looked back at him.

Johnnie looked up from the trunks of the trees to the night sky, and then back to his friend.

"I remember going down the trail with you. Getting hit. Pain. God-awful pain. You being next to me. We spoke, I asked you about the dog tags, and that's it."

Johnnie True Blood raised his hands to still Brian's voice before he could speak.

"Don't ask. I don't know. Don't know at all, but I'm loving each minute of this. Never felt like this. My whole body is electric. Peace, you know? You ever be at peace, Mac?"

Johnnie leaned back against a tall oak tree.

Brian reached for the whiskey bottle.

"Not that kind of peace. You don't want that. Answer my question, Mac."

"I need it."

"No you don't."

"No," Brian said curtly, "you don't know what I've been…"

Johnnie True Blood crossed his arms over his chest and embraced himself. He rolled to his side laughing. His torso was lit yellow and gold by the fire and his legs were in darkness.

"You can say that to me? You green mother. Why if it weren't for me, you'd be sitting here and I'd be sitting there. I taught you all the tricks of that trade."

The blood drained from Brian's cheeks turning them a pale white.

"Johnnie, I didn't mean…"

Brian looked down at the whiskey bottle in his hand.

"You did, but it don't matter. Besides, we got some talking to do and that whiskey won't help you."

"Talking?"

Johnnie True Blood smiled, pushed himself farther up against the tree, and crossed his arms over his chest.

"First question is why you went, Mac. Why did you go, Mac?"

Then, Johnnie True Blood clasped his hands together behind his head and leaned back against the trunk of a massive oak tree.

"After nine eleven…"

Johnnie True Blood chuckled and waved his right hand by way of interruption.

"You need to be honest with me, Mac. That's what we told everybody. Nine eleven. Patriotic. Serve our country. Others could understand that. We all had our reasons, but, Mac, why did you really go?"

Johnnie True Blood looked away from his friend to give him time to gather his thoughts.

Brian rose, and stood over the fire. He looked down at Johnnie True Blood.

"I...I..."

Johnnie True Blood looked up at his friend and waited.

"Yes?"

"What are you?" Brian asked. "Are you a ghost? A father confessor?"

"What do you need, Mac? A man like you, about to blow your brains out? What do you need, Mac?"

"How?"

"We gonna' be here a long time, Mac, you start asking how."

Johnnie True Blood burst out laughing. He rolled to his side, and then back, and looked at Brian.

"Hell, Mac, for all I know I was born yesterday."

Johnnie True Blood caught his breath.

"Oh, man, what do you need, Mac? The wisdom of a ghost?"

Johnnie True Blood pointed to himself. "Or, a father confessor? The confessional is open, no one in front of you, but god knows how many behind you."

Johnnie True Blood pointed to a large stone in the center of the clearing. Shadows of firelight flickered across it as waves on a beach.

Brian walked to the stone and sat. He slumped with his head in hands. Looking up, he saw Johnnie True Blood waiting patiently with a smile. Johnnie True Blood opened his hands as if to ask 'when?'

"The lieutenant split the platoon. Remember him? Hit the Forward Operating Base all fired up to get his CIB and go home a hero until we ran into that *falang.*"

Brian paused. He looked to Johnnie True Blood who nodded at him, and then Brian continued.

"I took a squad, you knew them all, with a platoon of Afghan regulars." Brian shook his head in disgust.

"If you can call them that. We kept one eye out for the Taliban and one eye on our allies. For all we knew they were the same thing. Our mission was clearing the road from our village to the marketplace. We had a Bradley in front, and six HUM-V's behind it, and a Bradley bringing up the rear. I was on the lead Bradley. Where I should have been, up front. Lead from the front. I knew what the mission was. We were supposed to clear the road. Clear the goddamn road. We climbed slowly up into the hills. One goddamn "S" turn after another slowing us down and making us targets. We couldn't have been doing more than three, four miles an hour. Even the fucking Afghans knew it was a shooting gallery. They never paid attention on patrols, but this day they were scared. They were really fucking scared. Or...."

Brian pointed his finger at Johnnie True Blood.

"...those bastards knew all along what was going to happen. The higher we climbed up the hill toward the marketplace the more nervous they got. Shit, Johnnie. You know. We didn't trust them. Watching them watching us. Hell, half of them were probably Taliban looking forward to collecting a bounty on our heads, or deserting, selling their gear, re-enlisting and doing it all over again. What the hell were we doing there? We shouldn't have been there. Afghans kept looking up at the ridges rising above us on both sides of the road like they knew what was coming. None of it felt right. We come around this one curve, and there in the road in front of us is a pile of rocks, a small pyramid, with a stick pointing out of the top of it with a note on it scribbled in whatever the fuck the language was they spoke in the valley. You remember that, Johnnie? They even had their own languages in some of those valleys. People born, lived, and died without ever leaving a valley, and we were going to make them safe."

Johnnie True Blood waved his forefinger in a circle.

"I'm getting there. Anyway, we could have run over the damn thing. Didn't need to stop. The interpreter jumped off the Bradley before I could say anything. He ran up toward the pile, picked up a stone, and then threw it at the pile. We all ducked expecting an IED, and that stupid sombitch to go flying back past us like Mary Poppins. Nothing happened. Somebody was looking down on that dumb sombitch."

Brian looked to the heavens.

"Allah? Buddha? Christ? Whatever or whoever else might be up there. The interpreter plucked the stick from the pile, and read the note as he walked back toward us sauntering like a buck private with his first month's pay on a Saturday night. 'Taliban say to villagers, stay off road. We kill all Americans and Afghan soldiers', he said and then crumpled it into a ball and tossed it away. I waved us on through. I gave the order to keep going up that goddamn road. We went past the rock pile; the HUM-V'S behind us went past.

The sharp crack of an explosion rolled overhead. Like a goddamn hand coming down from the sky pressing the air down on us. It pushed our chests in and took our breath. I turned and looked back. Our guys leaped out of the vehicles rolling onto the ground and firing into the rocks. Goddamn rounds going everywhere. Fifties opened up. M16's firing. All around me, men on their bellies firing into the rocks. Brass cartridge casings flying from the weapons, firing bursts. Afghan AK47's our M Sixteen's. Gray smoke rising around us. Down the road behind us thick, black smoke broiling out of the split belly of the Bradley. Crater in the road filled with oil. Yellow flames licking the skin of that fucking upside down beast. I could see, it was upside down! Screams. Our guys running down the road toward the Bradley, dropping empty magazines to the ground, jamming in loaded ones, and firing again. Gunners in the HUM-V's crouched behind thin metal plates, firing until the barrels of the machine guns glowed red. Somewhere to our front came the sound of their mortars close by. That goddamn hollow pop. A single plunk of the charge, sending the explosive round on a high arc toward us, so slowly you could see the dark shape reach the peak of its flight and then head

downward. Almost in wonder you watched the goddamn thing knowing full well it would blow your ass apart.

Then, it was over. Hands shaking we slipped the bodies of our
dead into dark body bags. The Red Cross emblem on the nose of
a Black Hawk suddenly appeared above us blowing dust, sand, and
pebbles into us. Closing our eyes and stinging our flesh. Empty litters
were tossed out one door by the crew chief while litters supporting
the wounded soldiers were carefully loaded from the other. The rotor
wash sent down a tornado of wind biting at our eyes and rippling desert fatigues. Then, I found Jenkins."

Brian lifted the bottle to his lips, waved his left hand at Johnnie
True Blood not to speak, swallowed hard, and then put the bottle
down.

"Jenkins was curled up in the shadow of a boulder, his legs drawn
up to his chest. Tiny, our medic got there first. You remember Tiny?"

Brian shook his head.

"Why is it that guys six foot six get the nickname 'Tiny'? He must
have carried a hundred extra pounds of medical supplies to compen-
sate for not carrying a weapon. He even volunteered to carry ammo
for the SAW, but you know we couldn't...When I got there Tiny was
kneeling by Jenkins giving him a shot of morphine. Tiny motioned
to me that he was giving him a second shot of morphine. He wasn't
going to make it and Tiny was killing the pain. Jenkins didn't know
where he was. He was dying and didn't know it. He was looking up
like a baby in a crib looking around. I guess he crawled or landed
over there. Does it matter how he got there? The blast shattered every
bone in his body. It was like he was one mass of jelly just held together
by his uniform skin. I crawled up to him and knelt.

I saw myself in his eyes. Jenkins's mouth trembled. He was trying
to find words, but couldn't. His lips were moving around but nothing
came out. The Bradley burned behind us covering us in smoke, small
arms rounds were popping off and flying over our heads. I bent low
to Jenkins. I held him. With everything he had left, Jenkins forced

one word through his blood-coated lips, Mommy. Three times he said that. Mommy, mommy, mommy. And why the fuck was I alive to hear that? Why? Why wasn't it me? I was on the first vehicle past the mine, it should have been me. Mommy, that's what he said with all the breath he had left in him, and then he died. What was he saying? Mommy, help me I'm dying? Mommy, I'm sorry for leaving you to be a soldier?"

Brian looked over his shoulder and then back to Johnnie True Blood.

"Was she a ghost like you? Was Jenkins talking to her? Mommy this motherfucker leaning over me killed me? I crouched there with his blood soaking me, and it didn't have to be. He didn't have to die. I was just sitting there confused as all fuck, just, I don't know what I was doing, and I realize a shadow is over me. I look up, and it's Lieutenant Colonel Collins, remember that asshole? You remember him? He was going to courts-martial you for wearing that amulet. Anyway, here he is, his Black Hawk had put down on the other side of the road. He drops a mine detector at my side. Looks at my oil and blood soaked fatigues and tells me he'll send me another set, and put me in for a Soldier's Medal. And then, with a glance down to Jenkins, he turns and leaves. That was it. We would have shot his goddamn Black Hawk down except that would have killed the crew. Collins was one of those assholes you knew would get out of there alive, get some stars on his shoulder, and be fighting the next goddamn war on the backs of other soldiers. Fucker was a politician. He wasn't a warrior like us."

Brian smiled.

"We just wanted to get the fuck out of there and get home, and Colonel Collins was afraid it was going to end. I found out later, the words that were garbled, that radio transmission from the lieutenant that I couldn't make out? What he said was if it doesn't feel right, don't go. We didn't have to go that day. It was up to me. My call. Jenkins and the others didn't have to die. Their deaths are on me, Johnnie."

"Perhaps. You don't look like a god to me, Mac."

Johnnie True Blood smiled. He raised his hands in mock protest. "Not that I've ever seen one."

He smiled.

"He would've made it home except for me," Brian protested.

"I don't believe that anymore than you do," Johnnie True Blood said with authority.

"We had two more days of us going up that road alone, Brian. Two more days of us being road bound targets. Shit, the guys fighting us had been defending that road from invaders since Alexander the Great. Their great grandfathers, the ones before that and the ones before that all the way back to the beginning of time. If you ain't from my tribe or valley, fuck you. You think they got it down pat by now? Run enough drills against the Russians, the Northern Alliance, and now us?"

Johnnie True Blood laughed softly. He pointed his finger toward the sky as if he were pointing toward the Taliban occupied ridge in his mind.

"The dudes up on top of that ridge were the same dudes we trained in the eighties to fight the Russians. The same assholes in DoD and State that armed them decades ago are trying to buy their loyalty now, and the brass are writing new books about the old strategies our uncles and fathers paid for in blood in the jungles, forgot, and we're paying for again. It's just an update of Hamburger Hill, that's all. All this new strategic brilliance is just the old bullshit in a new package with stars on the label."

Johnnie True Blood's voice grew cold.

"And you, you good hearted sombitch, you're going to carry guilt for Jenkins like some kind of penance?"

Brian opened his mouth and Johnnie True Blood waved him off.

Johnnie True Blood's tall form was bathed in the flickering light of the fire, shifting in and out of darkness. He looked down at Brian.

"How much luck does one man have? Get through one tour, maybe. Some don't. Get through a second tour? Some guys running out of luck there. Get through a fourth or fifth tour? No man's got that kind of luck. Got to be more to it than that. Don't you think?"

Johnnie True Blood shook his head.

"And you, you going to somehow put your bullet proof arms around Jenkins and keep him alive? You going to do every screaming thing right every moment of everyday even when you ain't been through it before?"

"No, not the way you make it sound."

"And how is that?" Johnnie True Blood said bending down until his eyes were level with Brian's. "Listen, what do you hear?"

For a moment Brian found himself looking through Johnnie's eyes at the trees behind his friend. Brian shook his head to clear his thoughts.

Johnnie looked up into the night sky. Brian followed Johnnie True Blood's lead and looked up at the scattered trail of the Milky Way stars across the black night, and listened to wind in the trees and the far off location calls of swirling hordes of brown bats. Then, it was very quiet.

"The woods?"

Brian was unsure of Johnnie True Blood's question, and more so of his answer.

"No," Johnnie True Blood said.

He reached for the bottle of whiskey and took a long swig out of it.

"Aaagh, why do you drink that?" Johnnie True Blood said.

He looked down at the bottle, and then back to Brian. He tossed the bottle to Brian who caught it.

"Still tastes as bad as it did when I was alive."

Johnnie took a deep breath.

"You're hearing time passing by, Mac. Time roaring past us, and there's nothing you can do to fight that stream. We sit here in this little eddy."

Johnnie True Blood reached out with his right arm bending at the elbow as if it were a paddle causing a silver, swirling white water eddy to appear in the air rushing around his elbow, "but it's swirling around us and then continuing on without end."

He raised his right hand as if removing it from the water, and the silver stream coursed out of the clearing and disappeared. He looked away as if he could see the eddy disappearing into the night.

"Just gone, Mac. Just gone. Maybe a few atoms from us get caught up in the swirl and go downstream. Maybe we splash the water a little."

Johnnie True Blood chuckled.

"Anything more than that and you've just got a very high opinion of yourself, your own worth."

Johnnie True Blood pointed up at the night sky.

"You see the Milky Way? Go ahead, look up there. Road map of time coursing through space as far as we can see? Been there long before you and I, and it's going to be there a long time after you and me. Stop it? I think not."

Brian was confused. Maybe Brian had already done it. Opened his mouth wide, tasted the acrid metal of the .45 causing his mouth to salivate, inhaled the pungent smoke, and felt a bullet tear through his brain. And then, darkness. Maybe he was as dead as Johnnie True Blood.

"You know why Jenkins's death hurts you so much?"

Johnnie True Blood raised his hands to silence potential protestations from Brian.

"I know, I was there, too. They all hurt. All of them. Part of us died with them. Scares the hell out of you, more likely the life. You ain't immortal anymore. Not even close. Gone."

Johnnie True Blood slapped his hands together, the impact a resounding clap, causing Brian to instinctively pull back. Johnnie smiled, and patted his right hand over his heart.

"Could have been me, but it wasn't, and let us all thank the Great Spirit for making us that way. Along with the guilt you're carrying of course. How many dead men's packs you carrying on your back filled with guilt?"

Johnnie True Blood looked to the night sky, and turned in a circle with his arms outstretched.

"We're hard wired to deny our own deaths. That's what they all tap into, duty, honor, country, god, and jihad. Young folks are already predisposed to go off and get their asses blown up. Prove something to the tribe. God or Darwin saw to that."

He looked down at Brian.

"People dead and dying all around, us maybe even next in line, but damn it we can sure deny it. How the hell else you think we get up each morning? Human beings good at denial. Sometimes too good. Man, that's a fuel for the engine of the soul. But, you, my friend, you want to know the reason Jenkins's death hurts you so much?"

Johnnie True Blood smiled.

"Hurts even now. Maybe more than it did that day?"

Brian found Johnnie True Blood's eyes barely inches before his own. Brian was no longer certain of what he was seeing. His knees felt weak.

"You've stopped time."

Johnnie True Blood laughed, and slapped his right thigh with his right hand. He pointed behind him and Brian instantly saw, perhaps was at once again, the remote dirt road running up that mountain in Afghanistan forsaken by the gods of the invaders.

The sun bleached bones of dead goats were scattered nearby where an errant dumb bomb had fallen into a farmer's fields before the F-16 pilot turned for home and a cold beer and clean sheets. The rusted hulk of a Soviet BMP armored personnel carrier, long since stripped of anything useful by the locals sat as a highway marker and a warning to the Americans.

"You're still there on that hill, Jenkins dying in your arms. The hissing sound of the fuel burning, that oily scent of it, the rumble of bits and pieces of words, and shouts, and screams, rounds popping off buzzing past your ears like bees, the touch of the sun on the back of your neck, the pattern of earth stains on your fatigues, you've stopped it all, in your mind. Each sight, sound, touch, taste, smell is embedded in you. Like a hundred tiny little land mines on the surface of your memories just waiting to go off at the touch of a sight or sound or taste or smell to take you back there. What you saw then is more real to you, fresher, than what you saw this morning. You never came home, Mac. You never went back to Barbara and Katie. You're still on that goddamn hillside. You choose to carry it with every atom of your body every day. You fool, I love you, Mac, but you're a fool. A fool with a big heart, and backpacks full of misplaced guilt."

Johnnie True Blood waved at the image of Jenkins' death and it faded from view.

"Guilt? You?"

Johnnie True Blood thrust his right hand through the air pointing at Brian.

"Guilt? You've got no guilt. Sombitch, you went! Motherfucker, you went! These millions of Sunshine Patriots we got us here at home? All these frigging great Americans who never heard a shot fired in anger or risked their family? Shit, we got politicians in office draping themselves in the flag who ducked the last war, but are happy to send you, and we got a new crop lying about going. Where the fuck were they when you were on that hill? They weren't standing alongside you. I don't remember seeing them with us."

Johnnie True Blood squinted.

"Hear me," he said softly.

"Deep inside that soul of yours that you got so twisted and tied up in knots. You don't carry no guilt for nothin'. You went. You stood. You took the fire and you did what you had to do. There's a more solid kind of honest to the bravery it took you to go then those bastards will ever know. It's that simple. I don't care how history judges it; whether it's right, or it's wrong, all I know is you had the guts to go. To put your ass on the line, and go."

Johnnie True Blood looked skyward, and then coursed his right hand through the air pointing at the valley. With his back to Brian he spoke.

"It's always been that fucking simple. If my ancestors what lived here could all come back, sit by this here campfire and smoke some tobacco with us, you think they wouldn't understand you?"

Johnnie True Blood shook his head, and looked to the east as if he could see the hillside in Afghanistan.

"Now, listen close, young trooper. None of that is there anymore. It's gone. Fly your ass back there and try to find it. Shit, go back and see if you can find the ones who did it. It was there for a moment, but you..."

Johnnie True Blood reached out in front of him, made as if to grasp something, and pull it to his heart.

"...you welded that moment to your heart, your soul. Time moved on."

Johnnie True Blood pointed overhead at the Milky Way; then made the swirling motion of a canoe paddle with his right arm causing the silver eddy to reappear in the air. Johnnie True Blood smiled a faint, straight line smile that was almost lost to Brian in the dim light of the fire.

"You ain't no god, Mac. You couldn't really stop time. You really can't stop things the way they were, and you couldn't stop Jenkins from moving on."

Johnnie True Blood smiled, nodded, looked away, and then back to Brian.

"You know, Mac, you never did answer my question. Why did you go, Mac? I had to run to the guns, and see what it was all about. All them stories from Henry Two Pines about his time in Vietnam, and his beer bellied buddies down to the Legion Hall. I had to see. I wasn't naïve, but I had to see if I measured up. What about you, Mac? You been ducking that question since you got home. You afraid to say why you really went? You wanted to know what it was like to kill someone? You one of those guys who needed to come back with rows of ribbons and prove you were somebody? You needed to know what you'd do when the shit happened? Family tradition? You couldn't not go? We all had a reason, a real reason, Mac. Before you pull the trigger of that pistol of yours you ought to fess up to what it was."

Jenkins, whole, safe, and smiling, his eyes looking directly into Brian's soul, emerged from behind Johnnie True Blood and made his way through the flickering light of the fire toward Brian.

Brian's body convulsed in spasms. He tried to rise, but his legs and arms collapsed underneath him. He tried to raise himself up with his arms and they proved to be weak and rubbery. Brian's throat was dry and tight refusing to let words rise from his soul.

"Here," Jenkins said with a broad smile as he reached down to Brian, "Let me help you up, Mac."

CHAPTER 7

GHOSTS

ONE HAS ONLY TO LOOK

*B*arbara, *wearing a bright yellow flower print summer dress, burst from the car, ran to the For Sale sign and stood jubilantly next to it. With her left hand she gestured toward Brian, and with her right she pointed at the house. A slight breeze tossed her long, brown hair over her shoulder. She paused seeing children yet to be born playing on the lawn. A gentle breeze tossed their hair as the young boy and girl ran with great Daisies twirling in their hands.*

"I give you our house," she said laughing.

The rush of adrenalin accelerated her heart rate. Her chest rose and fell.

Still wearing his desert camouflage fatigues from the week end drill, Brian walked slowly to Barbara and slipped his arm around her waist. His right hand pressed slightly against Barbara's abdomen.

"Okay," Brian said, "if this it, this is it."

"You sure?"

"Yeah," Brian said looking down at the folded paper with the listing. "We can afford it. Extra money from the Guard."

Barbara took a deep breath and pointed at the front of the house.

"Those shrubs have to go. We can put rhododendrons there. My mother always called them 'rodo-dodos'. Over there we can put a row of Azaleas."

Barbara walked on ahead with Brian trailing. And then, abruptly, she turned, walked back to Brian and embraced him. Burying her head against his shoulder, she sobbed.

"What? What?" Brian asked. "Why are you crying?"

"Brian," she pulled her head back from Brian's chest and looked into his eyes. "We have the house, we're having our baby, and I have you. And, we have each other."

She glanced over her shoulder at the house, and giggled.

"I don't care about azaleas as long as I have you. I will always have you? Won't I?"

The Tamarack Lodge sign was made of silver birch branches nailed over the screen door. The branches forming the letters were weathered to a pale gray by years of exposure to the elements. The bottom part of the "O" in Lodge was missing. None of the locals could remember when it fell off, but there was no great motivation to fix the sign. Everyone who needed to know where the Tamarack Lodge was already knew where it was. On either side of the sign was a ten point rack of white tail deer antlers. The building was a one story log cabin with dark green shutters open on both sides of the shoulder high windows. Tall pines surrounded the restaurant except for the one side faced with a square, gravel parking lot the size of a parade ground.

This was Monday, so Henry Two Pines was here to pick up whatever edible food was left over from the week end, and any other foodstuffs close to their expiration dates. Henry Two Pines leaned against the scarred front fender of his truck. Over the years, the fenders had taken on the appearance of having been banged with a ball peen hammer. The gnarled fingers of his right hand lingered in a dent caused by Johnnie True Blood and Brian when they'd had a few too many Genesee's on the way home one night and struck the gate on

Henry's road. There was character to Henry Two Pines' truck from each scar, dent, and scrape. Even if had the money, which he didn't, he wouldn't have traded the old truck in for a new one.

Henry wiped the sweat from his deeply tanned forehead with the back of his left hand. His skin was covered with purple blotches and his veins were dark and distended. Looking through the open door to the kitchen of the Tamarack Lodge he smiled at Claire Jagers sitting at the single, round table in the kitchen. Claire nodded to Henry.

"Thanks, Claire."

Henry Two Pines stepped back into the kitchen opening and pulling the screen door closed with a screech behind him.

"That leftover food will be more than welcome by those what get it."

"I wish it were more."

"What you give is appreciated, Claire."

"Shame it's us they have to depend on."

Henry Two Pines sat, and reached across the table touching Claire's hand. His fingers grazed the wedding ring that Claire still wore though her husband had passed many years before from old war wounds which never fully healed. Henry Two Pines' thoughts lingered on the agonizing way the old man died.

"They didn't have much before they lost him," Henry Two Pines said.

"They sure as hell don't have anything now. Uncle Sam has one cold heart toward the survivors and children."

Henry Two Pines and Claire looked toward the empty parking lot at the sound of screeching brakes and gravel striking trees. They jumped up from the table and went to the window.

An old van in a four wheel skid swerved across the gravel parking lot. Henry Two Pines caught a fleeting glance of a terrified woman clutching the steering wheel.

Barbara awoke at the sound of gravel striking metal like the strike of hail. She had the sensation of sliding across ice. Her fingers clutched the steering wheel struggling against the skid. Vainly, she fought for control. The front right tire slipped from the parking lot into soft earth. The van tipped, and then skidded on its side before striking a stand of old pines causing the airbag to fill. Darkness overwhelmed the driver. After a while, Barbara heard a voice.

"Miss, miss," Henry Two Pines said.

Barbara opened her eyes, sat up abruptly, and found herself on a cot in a small room. Defensively, she clutched her hands to her chest. She looked at the small man with the kindly face, and the older woman next to him. They seemed friendly. Moving her legs to the side of the cot she tried to stand up, but Henry Two Pines cautioned her not to.

"Where am I? Who are you? What happened to me?"

"Tamarack Lodge. You had an accident in our parking lot. You took a good shock from the air bag. Overall, you're pretty lucky. Car's banged up, but you seem okay. We ought to get you to a hospital?"

Barbara shook her head.

"No, no, I have to…"

The woman patted a cold, damp compress on Barbara's forehead.

"Claire Jagers."

She nodded.

"That's Henry Two Pines."

Barbara's brow furrowed at the sound of Henry Two Pines' name.

"He helped me get you inside. Dear, I think we ought to call an ambulance just to be safe."

"Oh no," said Barbara struggling to get to her feet.

"I've got to keep going, I've got to get to Speculator."

Barbara sat up feeling her legs and arms.

"I don't think I broke anything? I'm not bleeding?"

"Miss, that van of yours is not going anywhere, and I don't think you're in any shape to drive."

"But you don't know. I've got to…"

"I still think we ought to call an ambulance."

Claire looked at Henry Two Pines.

"Or, let us take you to the doctor's?"

Barbara got up from the cot, paused as if to make sure she was steady, and looked down at the others.

"Look, thank you very much, for what you did, but I have to get up there. Henry Two Pines? You? Johnnie True Blood? You know Brian?"

Barbara remembered the photograph of Brian and Johnnie True Blood holding freshly caught Lake Trout proudly before them, and Henry Two Pines standing behind them.

"Yes," Henry Two Pines said.

He rose, and extended both his hands to Barbara's and took hers.

"Barbara McAfee. You know where he went, don't you?"

Henry Two Pine's hand was electric to Barbara's touch.

"Yes."

"Will you take me?"

"Yes."

"First, we ought to get you something to eat," Claire said.

"I'm really not hungry."

"A cup of tea?"

"No, uh, okay."

Barbara suddenly felt weak, and sat in a chair at the table.

"And then we have to go. He might…"

Henry Two Pines nodded.

"Fine, you two go on in there and I'll get the tea. Henry?"

"Tea is fine."

Henry Two Pines opened the waiter's door connecting the kitchen to the dining room. Barbara entered.

"Anywhere," Henry said.

Inside, there was a small bar at the back of the room fronted by tall wooden bar stools, their seats polished smooth by years of the same patrons sitting in the same stools sliding on and sliding off. Over the years the soles of the patrons' shoes and the heels of their boots wore grooves in the chair rails. A dozen tables wore red and white vinyl tablecloths with plastic ketchup and mustard containers standing guard over dull cutlery and neatly folded paper napkins held in square aluminum containers. It was still in the empty bar and restaurant.

Barbara looked at the pine plank wall behind the bar. Two rows of black framed photographs were precisely spaced across the wall. Barbara looked at Henry who looked past her at the wall. Looking across the deserted bar Barbara made out the shapes of soldiers in the photographs, but not their faces. Barbara walked back to the bar.

"World War Two, Korea, Vietnam, Gulf War, Iraq, Afghanistan," Claire said.

She approached Barbara from behind.

"Folks from around here haven't missed a war since this country started."

She stood for a moment holding the two cups of tea, and then turned away and walked to the table where Henry Two Pines was sitting.

"All of them…killed?"

"Yes, dear. Hard luck and patriotism make for a lot of signing up. Not much work around here way that Albany tells what we can and can't do with the forest."

Claire placed the tea cups on the table, and then walked back to Barbara.

"I didn't…I thought…I mean…their families, too."

"My Billy," Claire said.

She pointed to a small photograph at the end of the line. She stepped to it, placed her hand on the photograph and then gestured at the bar wall beneath it.

"Looks like we're going to have to start another row."

Henry Two Pines nodded.

"I'm sorry," Barbara said.

"He was proud to serve."

Claire nodded.

"He wrote me from Basic Training about how proud he was. Funny it was, when they issued him all that brand new olive drab underwear. Said it made him feel like a soldier."

"Yes, maam," Barbara said.

Claire smiled.

"My other son just got back. Jeffrey. One of the other men, boy from Huntsville, Alabama in his unit isn't doing so well. Tried to hang himself before the neighbors stopped him. Jeffrey is down there, now, at his own expense trying to help him."

She shrugged.

"What can Jeffrey do?"

Claire's face suddenly contorted in anger.

"Army don't help them. Uses them up and sends them back hurt to us."

She looked deeply into Barbara's eyes.

"You'd think they'd try to fix them before they sent them home."

"I'm sorry," Barbara said.

"Have your tea, dear, before it gets cold."

Barbara sat at the table with Henry Two Pines and quickly drank her tea.

"Will you take me now?"

"Yes."

Henry Two Pines rose, and led the way from the restaurant. He looked back at the black and white photographs on the log wall, and then out to the parking lot. He held the door for Barbara. She paused stepping from the warmth of the restaurant into the chill air. Henry Two Pines held the door staring at Barbara wondering if she could see them.

"Yes?" Barbara asked.

"Nothing," Henry said. "Let's go."

CHAPTER 8

MUD WALLS AND BLACK HEARTS

DEATH OF A GOAT

Part Two of Parable: WHY DID YOU COME BACK?

*B*rian leaned back against sandbags stacked at the entrance to his squad's bunker. His back ached and his knees throbbed in pain. He couldn't hide his difficulty in rising after resting anymore. His upper torso covered in shade, and his legs thrust into the bright sunlight, Brian patiently loaded one 5.56mm round after another into a magazine for his M-4 carbine. He patted his fatigue shirt pocket, felt the still sealed letter from Barbara, and shook his head. After the last letter from her, bemoaning her loneliness and isolation, and the hardship in raising Katie alone, Brian knew better than to read it in his current state. God help him if Johnnie or somebody else found some alcohol and Brian got good and liquored up and went on line again and called Barbara.

Just get through the fucking day, thought Brian. Just get through this fucking day and get into tomorrow. Wake up with both arms and legs.

Suddenly, Brian was overcome with despair. He was dizzy, and clutched the earth as if to keep from toppling over. Rolling to his side, Brian crawled on all fours into the dark bunker. Feeling for his sleeping bag he reached inside and pulled out an olive drab towel. Forcing the terry cloth towel, pungent with his own scent, against his face, Brian sobbed. He fought to lower the sound of his cries lest the others hear.

Johnnie True Blood's tall shape filled the opening to the bunker. He reached down toward his friend. His hand stopped mere inches from Brian's shoulder, and then Johnnie True Blood pulled it back, turned, and closed the crude door to the bunker.

And then, it was over. Wiping the tears from his eyes one last time, Brian turned to rejoin his squad as he suddenly knew that he was crying over the death of the goat.

Brian shifted his weight uneasily sitting before the fire. How could he believe what he was seeing and hearing? Was he in an alcohol induced stupor lying somewhere in a sterile hospital under some white suited doctor's care? Were their care givers around him sticking IVs and drugs into his blood stream? Had he finally over-dosed on booze? Part of him struggled against the calming influence that Johnnie True Blood had on him. How could he accept Johnnie True Blood? He was dead! How could he be sitting here talking to him as if they were back at Camp Crusader or having a brew at a stateside NCO Club? But, there he was. Like it was yesterday? And Jenkins? Brian looked around.

"I tell the story and Jenkins is here?"

"And?" Johnnie asked.

"And, what?" Brian shook his head.

"What?"

"How the fuck can you be here? How the fuck can we be having this conversation?"

"You came to me," Johnnie True Blood said.

Johnnie waved his right hand in an open, rolling, invitational way, and smiled.

"I was just sitting here minding my own business."

"You know what I'm talking about. For God's sake, Johnnie you're dead!"

"So?"

"I see you for Christ's sake!"

"Is this a game, Mac?"

Johnnie smiled.

"I see you, too."

The smile on Johnnie True Blood's face turned into a scowl.

"Mac, you want to play fucking paddy cakes with me, or you going talk to me? You got a shot at redemption here before you blow your brains out."

"How do…?

Johnnie True Blood nodded to the green bag by Brian's feet, and then shook his head.

"We're way past the point of you questioning anything, Mac."

Brian took a deep breath.

"Lieutenant Osborne and Sergeant Cryers got taken out by snipers. One right after the other. They just let us come in, and then took them out."

Brian's words were interspersed with hisses and snaps from the fire growing louder. Intertwined red and yellow ribbons of flame twisted like serpents locked in a struggle to the death.

"Then, all hell broke loose. Shit, it was a fucking melee."

He turned away from Johnnie True Blood to stare at the hills shrouded in night. His breath came hard and heavy.

"Good, good," Johnnie True Blood said, "a fucking melee, go on."

He waved his hand again, and leaned back against the wide oak.

"We were backed up against one of those long, high mud brick walls which ran the whole length of the town. Every goddamn one of those hamlets was just one big bunker. Across the street Taliban are firing at us from the roof top of an old building. Fearless mother fuckers looking to die and claim their virgins. How the hell you gonna' fight somebody wanting to die and go to those virgins by an oasis? Sombitch ain't got nothing to live for and everything to die for. Their whole promotion system is stacked against us. Those bastards standing up to get a good angle and shooting down at us. Bullets popping into those goddamn bricks. Pieces of mud and dust and brick flying all over. No goddamn place to hide."

Sweat poured down across Brian's forehead, and his back. His heart pounded and his throat was dry. He continued looking away from Johnnie True Blood, and then turned, walked back to the fire, and sat near his friend.

"They shifted their fires to both ends of our line."

Brian shook his head.

"Started walking their fire in. They were trying to herd us into one spot. Probably send some asshole with a suicide vest into us. Everybody was getting hit. Some guys more than once. The lieutenant was gone."

Brian smirked.

"Fucking lieutenant was going to make the world safe for democracy. Help those Afghans build a nation. Lead some fucking crusade or something. Sniper got him right between the eyes. Blew the back of his head out like a yellow mushroom cloud over their dirt. Still had that tiny version of the New Testament stuck in the pocket of his body armor. Platoon sergeant gone. That sombitch was worth something." Brian cried. "Sergeant Cryers. That sombitch, I…."

"You said that. You're stalling."

"I had no choice."

"You did. There's always a choice, man. You're just shitting yourself now, and you can't shit me."

"I didn't have a choice."

"Man, do it. It ain't gonna' get any easier."

"Batteries ran out for the night vision gear. Blind as bats we were. Watching the muzzle flashes ripple along the top of the roof. Taliban just pouring on the fire. They weren't too fucking accurate but they knew how to pull a trigger. Streams of green tracers coming down from the building. Bouncing back up like fireworks. So many god-damn bullets my ears were buzzing. Like swarms of bees. It didn't look like there were any civilians around."

"You didn't care," Johnnie True Blood said.

"No, we didn't, did we? At that fucking moment anything that moved was Taliban. Sort the shit out afterwards and let some officer go pay off the family and express regrets. I was just a ser-geant. Why should I care how many fucking civilians died? Nobody else did? Nobody, not the brass, not the media, not the folks back home?"

Brian rose, turning away from Johnnie speaking over his back at him.

"We didn't see, hear, or smell them. We couldn't have."

"I ain't convinced. You ain't either."

"All right! I did it! Two F sixteen's came in with five hundred pounders. Danger close. I had to talk that flight leader into doing it. He didn't want to take the responsibility for hitting us. I took it."

Brian turned in a circle and stopped. He looked at Johnnie True Blood.

"I didn't do it none of us were getting out of there."

"Yeah," Johnnie True Blood laughed. "Them or us. God, I've heard that before."

"You were one of us, once!" Brian shouted.

"That cut deep, Mac. All things considered."

"I'm sorry."

"Go on, Mac."

Brian looked to the night sky as if he were suddenly back there.

"You couldn't hear or see them. The earth trembled. Vibration traveled up our legs. Shook us. The blast wave lifted us up and smashed us against that mud wall. Guys fell back to earth leaving blood stains on the wall where their bodies had been."

Brian shook his head.

"Shook us around like some mother bitch grabbing her pups at the neck by the teeth and snapping them around. Clouds of dust glowed in the fires where the building had been. It was like the air was a glowing, living being eating the dead."

Brian paused.

"Houses on both sides of the target were gone. Punched flat. Dust, and steam, and smoke rising. Then we heard it."

Brian shook his head.

"Heard them. Those goddamn moans and screams."

Brian trembled.

"I hear them now," Johnnie True Blood said softly.

Brian cocked his head toward a soft breeze from the east.

"I haven't stopped hearing them!"

Brian shook his head as if he were a swimmer trying to force water from his ears.

"I've never stopped hearing them."

Brian took a deep breath.

"Firing stopped."

Brian's voice went low, and he spoke sharply.

"They were gone. All of them."

Brian looked to the night sky.

"Probably up there somewhere with those seventy two virgins looking down on us and laughing."

Brian shook his head and looked to Johnnie. Johnnie stared back at him providing no relief.

"We got every swinging sombitch. All of them."

Brian pointed at the night sky.

"Sitting around an oasis eating dates and drinking cool pure water in the company of virgins."

"We all got to believe something, Mac," Johnnie True Blood added.

He stared up at the Milky Way as if he too sought to see the fallen Taliban and their reward.

"There she was."

Brian looked down at the ground, and gestured with his right hand. Her image was as real to him that moment as it had been so many months before.

"She was missing her right arm and right leg. Her little bur'qa was red with her blood. Clenched in her left hand. Face set in pain; numbed by shock. Her severed right arm lay by her. Her goddamn hand was tight in a fist! Must have been her last gesture shaking her fist at the heavens and her tormentors. At us. I think she was mouthing 'fuck you' at me but no words came out. She was cursing me. Didn't matter if it was English or Pashto. Or some frigging language only the people in the valley knew. Some curse handed down across the generations who'd fought all the invaders. Lying next to her was a young boy. Her brother I guess. Maybe six or seven. Black eyes like cold lumps of coal. He stared right at me. Looked at his sister and then me. Made like he was firing an AK at me. Christ, Johnnie they got more generations of mujahidin in the pipeline in that damn country than we got bullets."

"I know," Johnnie True Blood said. "You got our ass over there."

Brian started to protest, but Johnnie True Blood waved him off.

"No, Mac, I ain't blaming you, but as I recall you were the one who wanted to make a few more bucks to get that house with Barbara. You convinced me what a grand idea it would be for us to go into the Guard. That's how it went down, Mac. I ain't blaming you, Mac for the way I came home anymore than you can blame yourself for anything that happened over there. It just happened, Mac."

Johnnie True Blood paused.

"Until they shipped me home the way they did. You came home."

Johnnie True Blood smiled.

"Why, Mac? Why did you come home? You could have just as easily done over there what you're planning on doing here tonight. Hell, you could have done it in a firefight, gone out a hero, and no one would have ever known the pain you were in." Johnnie rose, and stepped out of the circle of light surrounding the fire and disappeared into the darkness.

"Hey, where are…"

A child covered from head to toe in a pale green bur'qa stepped from the darkness into the fire light. Two delicate hands reached out from under the bur'qa and pulled back the top revealing the young girl's long black hair combed back and tied with a thin, yellow ribbon. Looking directly at Brian she brought her hands from behind her back stepping completely into the light. She stepped toward Brian extending her arms.

Brian stepped to her. Their hands touched as Brian collapsed to the ground, his forehead resting on the girl's sandals; his tears cleansed her skin.

CHAPTER 9
LAND OF THE PASHTUN
Pain Feels Good

Part Three of Parable: DO YOU WANT TO LIVE OR DIE?

O lder Afghani men sat in the shadows of entrances to the mud brick homes in the village. No women or girls were visible. Brian's platoon moved cautiously down both sides of the narrow main road which led through the village. Brian's squad was in the lead and Brian was walking point. Lately, his back and knees had caused him pain after several hours of carrying a heavy pack. In a perverse way, the pain felt good to him.

He tensed as he walked past the doorways searching for any sign of weapons or a threat. Looking up the dirt road and along the high walls he knew that danger was all around him. The only sound he heard was that of the soles of his boots against the loose pebbles in the dirt road. Then, he heard the lone male voice, and the chanting refrain of young children. As he made his way deeper into the village the sound grew louder. Turning a corner, he stepped into the open air madrassah.

A single male teacher stood before perhaps twenty children ranging in age from six to thirteen. Brian assumed than anyone older was carrying a weapon for *one side or the other. Brian signaled with his left hand to those behind him to stop. He looked upon the neat rows of children. His eyes made contact with one young boy. Pure, ugly hatred was in the dark eyes of this one staring directly at Brian. So, thought Brian, how many years before you've got an AK in your hands?*

The fire burned low with a soft hissing sound of moisture in the wood heated to steam escaping in white puffs ascending to the night sky. Johnnie True Blood reappeared waving at Brian to continue speaking.

"We were all hard mothers; or at least we thought we were. That was probably our first mistake. We thought we'd seen just about everything there was to see."

Brian laughed softly and took another pull on the bottle of Bourbon.

"We'd all lost friends. Didn't talk about it. We'd all lost our nerve a time or two and one of the others pulled us through. We didn't talk about that either. I mean, after a while you didn't get up from a shit when the mortars came in, you know, just knew when the time came it was coming, and there wasn't a fucking thing you were gonna' do about. We were all dead, we knew that. Somehow it just made it easier when we stopped worrying about it. I mean, I didn't want to lose an arm or a leg, but I stopped making plans for after. We never said, you know Johnnie, if we said it, it somehow sealed the deal, and maybe, just maybe we had a shot to get out. But, this..."

Brian took another sip. Johnnie nodded.

"I heard later there were six SF guys out this time. We only found five. Somehow, the Taliban had taken them alive. You remember. You took point. Around us, the rock walls of the canyon rose up so steep you couldn't see what was up on top. Scared the fuck out of me climbing up that ridge. Funny. I wasn't afraid of dying I was afraid of heights. We crested that ridge, and came into a small gully. The earth was soft and you could see imprints; boots, smooth depressions where men had been forced down against the earth and dragged. Looking at the gouges in the earth, you could almost hear the screams of the struggle that took place there. U.S. gear, canteens, harnesses, tossed aside. Boots…"

Brian's voice grew deeper.

"Some jihadist sombitch had taken their boots and lined them up in a row, like we did at memorial services. Them bastards didn't miss a trick. You could see where their legs and boots were dragged to the stakes them jihadists had driven into the ground. The ground was brown with blood. A couple hours old."

Brian swallowed hard. He squinted and took a deep breath.

"Gutzman went to the first one. He didn't have a face, Johnnie."

Brian clenched his teeth; his jaw muscles tight. He spit each word out of his mouth.

"He…didn't…have…a…face. Gutzman looked down at the corpse and back to me. You know, for a second, I thought I saw emotion on Gutzman's face, and then all I saw in his eyes was steel. He was one hard mother. The Taliban had smashed the bones of this soldier's face with AK47 rifle butts until all that was left was fleshly pulp. You couldn't even tell where his eyeballs had been. His fatigue shirt was ripped open. They used tribal Choora daggers to thrust through his ribs and into his heart. God knows how long it took…then; Gutzman reached up where the man should have had a neck, and gently pulled out the bloody chain of his dog tags. He read it to us. It was suddenly so silent on the hill top that we heard Gutzman's words. Osborne, Richard G.

Gutzman was as calm as a padre at a baptism. You know, Johnnie he had a different gear he'd shift into times like that. Remember? He reached back, and I stepped up, raised my hand, and let him drop the bloody steel ovals onto my palm. Gutzman moved to the next man. I told you, old Gutzman always knew what to do. They were bodies now, not friends. We were alive. At least for the moment, and trying to do the right thing by them.

The next one was stripped completely naked. Shrapnel scars on his chest. Sometime back he'd taken an AK round through the fleshy part of his right arm. They must have wanted him to watch Osborne die. They cut his balls out with a dagger, and placed them on the earth next to him. Ripped him open and left him to die. The muscles of his jaw were set to when the last cry of pain or scream of rage had come out. Fucker passed in torment. Jesus.

Gutzman bent down to collect the second dog tag. Watts, James J., Gutzman said to me. Behind me, the others in our squad formed a ragged line of respect while keeping their eyes above us and below us on the hillside. No telling where those bastards were. I took his dog tags as well. I watched Gutzman's shoulders quake as he moved to the third soldier. Gutzman's hands were trembling. He had the shakes, but nothing was going to stop him. It was getting to him, Johnnie. If it got to Gutzman, man you know it had to be something. You want brave, Johnnie?"

Brian's voice choked with emotion, tears flooded his eyes, and his hands trembled with the bottle clutched hard between them.

"That's brave. Covered in blood from his knees down, sweat, and the brown dust of that goddamn place caking his chest, Gutzman stepped to the next one. A tall man, this one. Had the look. A southerner no doubt. His generation's turn with a rifle, no doubt. Revolutionary War. Civil War. The World Wars. I bet all his uncles had gone. Probably stood around the barbecues on the 4th of July all scarred up in their shorts. The jihadists slit him from the sternum to his balls; his guts hung down across his lap. Gutzman's voice broke when he spoke this time. Jennings, Walter E. Next to the body, was a rectangular flap of skin, the flesh dried from hours exposed to the air, and the bottom dark, brown. I looked down at the "AA" tattoo of the 82nd Airborne, All American division. Sons of bitches had sliced his airborne tattoo from his arm. What kind of mind thinks that way? They aren't like us, Johnnie."

Brian took another swig of bourbon.

"Gutzman moved on to the next soldier. The Taliban must have grown tired when they got to him. Single round from a K54 pistol in the forehead. Black hole through the bone. Back of his head blown off and his brains scattered on the hillside. Jefferson, Calvin G., Gutzman said. The last one must have been the patrol leader.

They'd taken their time with him. Long deep cuts to his arms and chest. They really wanted to have him suffer. Blond, blue eyed, crew cut, tanned. They must have killed the others before him. Peters, Harold I. Gutzman handed me the last dog tag. I put it with the rest. Gutzman had no words. Turning around, I watched Tiny. You remember Tiny, our medic."

Brian cried, and the crying became uncontrollable sobs. He fought to speak through his tears.

"These guys were dead and here comes Tiny. I don't know if he was out of his mind, or what. Fuck, by that time which one of us wasn't out of his mind. One by one, he's bandaging them up. Cleaning them up. Gutzman wanted to stop him, and I said no, let him go. Oh, God, let him go. The enemy hated the SF guys. They come in see what's happening, take somebody out, or snatch and grab somebody, or call an air strike. Pay a bounty to the locals for turning them in. Well, they got this bunch. Tied them down. Stripped them."

Brian turned away from Johnnie True Blood looking at the panorama of his memory against the night.

"I see the blank stares in their eye. I see every strand of hair on their heads. I see the caked blood on their arms and legs. I see their balls sliced from one and lying on the earth next to him. I see everything I saw that day sharper today."

Brian wiped the tears from his eyes. A thin, hard smile appeared on his face. His eyes squinted hard and narrow.

"Then, Gutzman pointed down at the trail, and then up the hillside. First Platoon was coming down the hill with six Taliban prisoners. They had their arms restrained behind their backs with plastic straps. Tall bastards these guys were. Like Osama. And the looks on their faces as they neared us. Defiant motherfuckers. These sombitches weren't afraid of anything or anyone. Gutzman pointed at them, and then to the bodies. We knew it was them, and we waited for them to come to us. We let First Platoon pass through us and then we stepped between First Platoon and took their prisoners. The rest was all she wrote."

Brian's smile vanished. For a long pause Brian was back on that hillside at that moment.

Johnnie True Blood looked up from the fire to the night sky arrayed with the brilliant path of the Milky Way.

Behind Johnnie True Blood emerged a single Taliban, Choora dagger tucked in his belt, his burning eyes upon Brian.

Brian turned; saw the Taliban, and Brian's right hand sought the M4 carbine which was no longer within reach. Behind the Taliban, Brian saw the faces of the five other jihadists he and Gutzman and the others had executed that day on the ridge. The other Taliban held back within the black folds of shadow of the dark woods.

Brian walked slowly to the Taliban, and as he did so all of the tall man's physical features faded away until there was just a wisp of memory of them in Brian's mind's eye. The features of the Taliban's face were now indeterminate except for brilliant orbs burning with intense silver light in the sockets of his skull.

Brian stared at the faded brown tunic-shirt, sheepskin vest, and pants. The clothes hung in the air as if they were a scarecrow in a farm field. There was no substance to this apparition. Brian reached through the tunic-shirt to where the man's heart would have been feeling only the cold night air.

"It's your call, Mac. Do you want to live or die?" Johnnie True Blood laughed. "I never got to that point. Choice was made for me, but you get to make the call for the rest of your life. Gonna' be minutes, or years, Mac? You gonna' reach into that pack and end it, or go back down that hill. Back to Barbara and Katie?"

CHAPTER 10
ALCHEMY
Swords Into Plowshares

*B*rian's dream form attempted to turn away from those before him. His body vainly fought against the damp sheets in an attempt to gain traction and run. The first row wore the dull pale brown and white washed out, desert fatigues of American soldiers. The second line wore the traditional robes of Pashtu tribesmen, and faded canvas bandoliers containing 7.62mm rounds for AK-47's. Several mujahedin had rocket propelled grenade launchers propped casually over their shoulders.

Brian walked uneasily among them. Soldiers armed with rifles slung over their shoulders, grenades hooked to their harnesses, stood ready. Each man held his head within the cradle of his right arm; stoic facial expressions all.

It never changes, thought Brian, no matter how many times I do this. Brian walked to the second line, reached out to the Taliban fighter, and accepted the AK-47 assault rifle. This soldier's eyes were the hollowness of cave entrances with darkness disappearing into the interior. Brian inspected the breech, allowed the bolt to slam forward, and returned the rifle to the soldier. Slowly moving through the viscous, glowing air, currents of light twisted in *eddies around Brian. The light wove a pattern of rivulets through the valley. Brian stopped, attempting to stand at attention, before Osborne, Jenkins, and Jefferson, and Peters, but was unable to control the tremors in his arms. Osborne spoke first. "They're the ones." He nodded to the Afghans. Jenkins, Jefferson, and Peters blinked their eyes. Brian felt the touch of human flesh within his palm. He knew not to look; all his instincts screamed silently within his skull not to look, but he did. Atop the familiar black ridge at the edge of the plain cast in gold; a deep blue sky shocked with electric, gold filaments, stood the shapes. Jenkins, the girl, the Special Forces patrol, the Taliban, they were all here.*

"More?" Johnnie True Blood asked.

He smiled and stared intently at Brian, and then waved his right arm as if wrapping the night around him like a cloak.

"More?" Brian responded.

Brian turned, walked to the green pack, and removed the .45 automatic pistol. He hefted the .45 automatic in his right hand tilting the barrel to look down it as if to make sure the round was still in the chamber.

Johnnie True Blood looked at the gun. His flesh stung with remembrance of the wrist jamming impact of the steel grip learning to control the power of the weapon within his grasp.

"Still comfort you?" Johnnie True Blood asked.

"I…"

"Yes? Taking too long, pal."

Johnnie True Blood arched his eyebrows.

"I don't believe you. I don't believe you believe yourself."

"You're fading?"

Brian moved closer to Johnnie True Blood reaching out toward him.

"Am I?"

Johnnie True Blood smiled looking through his arms at the gnarled trunks of tall pines, through his legs and feet at the pine needle covered forest floor, and then grinning as he looked back at Brian. Johnnie True Blood nodded.

"You've got to take it the rest of the way. It's all yours now. I always did carry you."

Johnnie True Blood faded even more. He laughed.

"Showed you how to pack your ruck. What to carry, what not. How to move. I even came to this place before you. God, Mac, I wish I had a friend like me."

"For the love of god, Johnnie…" Brian pleaded.

"God?" Johnnie True Blood shouted.

"God?"

Johnnie's form momentarily regained its intensity. He was barely inches in front of Brian. He laughed.

"You don't need me anymore, Mac."

Johnnie True Blood burst into loud haunting laughter reveling in the sense of his being.

The earth beneath Johnnie True Blood and Brian trembled. Branches on nearby trees shook, and startled birds suddenly took to flight. A brisk breeze rose up and swept over them tousling the hair on their heads and tugging at their shirts. A grin of pure joy was on Johnnie True Blood's face.

Johnnie True Blood rose above the ground, turned in a slow circle with his arms outstretched.

"Ah, Brian. I feel."

He sighed.

"Air in my lungs."

He inhaled deeply savoring the pressure of the air against his lungs. He looked down at his hands.

"Even the touch of the fire."

He looked skyward, and then to the woods, and finally at the ground.

"I'll miss this. You know, I don't know where it is."

"Where what is?"

Brian was startled at the prospect of his friend's departure.

"I don't want you to leave. Where what is?"

"The spirit world."

Johnnie True Blood looked away from Brian at the valley below and the hills surrounding them.

"This was just a stop along the way. For you, man, and for me."

Johnnie True Blood moved to his friend, and stopped. He towered over him.

Brian looked up through his friend's face to the visible pin points of Orion's belt.

"You can't..." Brian protested.

"Paddling in the Milky Way," Johnnie True Blood laughed.

Noticing Brian's stare, Johnnie True Blood looked over his shoulder.

"Yeah, we were warriors, once, Brian. We're not anymore. You've got bigger things to attend to now. You can't stay me, my course, any longer, Brian. You know that. Always was saving your ass. Now, it's your turn."

Johnnie True Blood turned away, paused, and then turned back to Brian.

"The great mystery was why any of us lived and others died. That will always be the mystery, Brian. Don't look for more to it than there is. There was no logic for it you and I will ever know. The guilt. We'll have that forever. The guilt for coming home is acid corroding your soul. Don't look for a purpose."

Johnnie True Blood laughed softly.

"Purpose finds you. Just like it found me. So long, my friend."

Brian barely saw Johnnie True Blood's form against the backdrop of night. Brian stared intently as if by the power of his will he could indeed delay the departure of his friend. Then, Brian could no longer see Johnnie True Blood's shape. Only two reflective pinpoints remained where Johnnie True Blood's eyes had been. And then, Brian found he was no longer even looking at them.

Brian was alone now. He slumped back against a tall pine tree. More alone than he had ever been, but he was not fearful. There was no anger in his heart. His head fell to his chest as if suddenly overcome by sleep after days without its comfort. With great effort, Brian raised his head. Holding the .45 out in his right hand, he watched it slowly turn to dust, and the dust pour from his palm to the earth where it soon disappeared in the bed of pine needles on the forest floor. Brian's hand rose as the weight of the gun diminished.

With his left hand, Brian up-ended the open bottle of Bourbon watching the amber liquid soak into the dry earth like fresh blood into desert sand. Drip by drip it fell to the earth.

There was a time when I would have lied, stole, or killed for that much whiskey.

Brian rose inhaling the cool night air as if he could taste it. He heard minute crackles of sparks in the fire. He saw tiny black shapes flit overhead in the black sky against the brighter pattern of stars. He felt the cool fingers of the night breeze touch his skin. The fragrance of all life in the valley was rich.

Every aspect of his being resonated in a harmony and peace he had never known. He wanted for nothing. He ached from nothing. There was bliss to his being.

He patted his arms and legs as if checking for wounds, and then rose to begin the trek back toward the road.

Stepping from the light of the fire into the darkness, suddenly feeling a chill, Brian turned as if to catch the last echo of the words from his friend. Then, he looked toward the trail revealed in the starlight and headed back toward the road.

CHAPTER 11
REDEMPTION
Unconditional Love

*T*he wail of a creature tearing itself apart from the inside out echoed from the ridge top. The wail was backed by a chorus from dimly discernible creatures shimmering in the distance. The soldiers standing by Brian fixed their heads upon their necks, and un-shouldered their rifles at the distant scream. The eyes of each of the specters glowed hot, and yellow. Apparitions jumped through the pale blue night turning somersaults and swinging enormous double-edged swords. Swarms of bullets flew like bees around Brian. The air pressed against his skin as the bullets passed. The distance closed. Rifles smoked oil with hot barrels and grips hard to hold but harder still to set down. Swords slashed through bodies, arms, and limbs cracking bones and carving flesh. Arms and legs flew from the defenders.

A grotesquely distorted image of Brian's face, mere inches from his own, looked down upon him. Brian shouted his horror at the recognition, but no words escaped from his mouth. A glowing, gold blade neared his neck only to be stayed. A macabre laugh assaulted his ears.

The demon bowed in flight, and then soared into the darkness above. Brian turned completely around. He was once again alone. He heard laughter as he stared into blinding light filling his vision. Slowly, he saw Johnnie True Blood emerge before the intense background of white light. Brian saw the outline of his friend's shape.

Brian stared into the grinning face of his friend. Brian's eyes blinked reflexively. He smiled. Brian tried to speak, but he had no words. He tried to nod that he indeed did see Johnnie True Blood, but the others were there as well. Brian struggled to move though he could no longer feel his body. He was helpless. The others gathered behind Johnnie True Blood were barely touched by the light. In a moment they would be upon him. Brian would be back in their realm. The specters moved as if to pass around Johnnie True Blood, and he moved to block them. Johnnie True Blood smiled, and waved to Brian. "Tap dancing......"

Brian couldn't tell if Johnnie True Blood had spoken, or if Brian had read his lips, or Brian just knew what Johnnie was saying. The words came to Brian. "...in the shadow of death..."

Then, Brian's thought trailed off into a deep sleep no longer beset by nightmares.

Off to the east the stars were fading against a lightening night sky. Hint of the sunrise soon to be upon them appeared as a reddish gold hue just above the horizon. The thick forest lining both sides of the narrow asphalt highway shifted from a monolithic dark wall into uncountable trees standing shoulder to shoulder.

Henry Two Pines slowed his old pickup and turned off the asphalt highway to the macadam road. The truck bucked and bounced down the narrow track, over rain moistened ruts, and then he parked it in the small lot at the trail head. It was incredibly quiet as he turned off the engine. There was no wind in the trees. No birdsong. Henry Two Pines looked at Barbara. Her back was to him.

The parking area was square with tall stands of trees abutting it on all sides allowing for only the narrow road to penetrate the forest and reach it. Knee high logs lay parallel to the ground atop other log cylinders framing the parking lot. A rain stained wooden sign, its words unreadable at that distance, no doubt showed the trailhead and provided cautionary warnings to the day hikers. No other cars were there.

The sun slowly crested the tree line of the horizon casting weak sunlight up the road Henry Two Pines and Barbara had just driven. The sunlight fell on the narrow road in a long, pale red hue, and then spread across the earth of the parking lot.

Barbara and Henry Two Pines sat silently in the truck. She felt a lonely stillness to this place as she got out of the car, careful not to slam the door, and closing it gently behind her. Henry did as well. They looked to each other in a mutual understanding of the sanctity of a hallowed place. Henry Two Pines smiled at Barbara and nodded toward the trail head. Barbara returned the smile, started for Henry Two Pines who waved her away, and then she walked quietly across the parking lot.

As Barbara moved away from the truck toward the trail head Henry Two Pines stayed back leaning against the truck. He had honored Brian's wishes the day before. This morning he honored her wishes. Henry Two Pines knew that whomever or whatever would emerge from that trail would complete the story.

Barbara's eyes fixed on the trail where it led from the lot into the woods. Deep shadows beyond the lip of the parking lot prevented her from seeing inside the woods. She stood still in the chill autumn air looking at the trail leading into the dark woods, and then looked back at Henry Two Pines.

"How would Henry Two Pines know to find Brian here?" Barbara said softly to herself.

"Why this place?"

She looked up at the tall pines bathed in the red hue of the sunrise.

Barbara's words were cut off abruptly at the sound of a voice booming out of the woods accompanied by the clatter of branches striking branches. From silence the forest had burst into life. The sun rose higher and the red hue filled the clearing below. Then, Barbara recognized the voice, made out the words, and stepped toward the trail. She clutched her hands together in front of her breast.

"You had a good home, but you left!" Brian's voice boomed. "You're right! You had a good woman but you left. You're right! Jody was there when you left. You're right! Sound off, one two, sound off, three, four, sound off, one, two, three, four. You had a good girl, but you left! You're right! Sound off! One, two, three, four!"

Brian burst from the woods like a cloud of steam rushing from a geyser. He seemed younger to Barbara. His body was cast in the dawn's pale red hue before the backdrop of the dark ranks of the forest. His skin shone a white purity of hue. His eyes were two brilliant points. His hair was disheveled; his clothes dirty, but he appeared beatific with a great grin stepping from darkness into light and pausing before Barbara. There was an eagerness and vibrancy to his movements that Barbara remembered from his past. He seemed as he was before all of this, the war, what had happened between Brian and Barbara. Brian's head snapped back and he grinned immensely at the sight of Barbara. He opened his arms wide.

Suddenly he became self-aware of his appearance, and brushed dust, dirt, leaves, and twigs from his shirt. He grinned with a boyish look Barbara had not seen since their teenage years in Speculator.

Barbara clasped her face. Her eyes met Brian's. Slowly and deliberately he walked toward her. Barbara hesitated as Brian closed the distance between the two of them. She looked over her shoulder at Henry Two Pines to make sure she was still in her reality, that this was all real, and she was seeing what she saw at that moment. Before she could think Brian reached her and embraced her. Turning to Brian, Barbara held him tight. She felt his warm tears streaming down her cheek mixing with hers falling together.

"Barbara, I'm sorry. Sorry for it all."

"Me too, I'm sorry, so sorry."

Brian kissed Barbara on the neck and she pressed her head hard against his shoulder.

Brian laughed softly and smoothed Barbara's tear touched long hair from her face.

Brian gently pushed Barbara away from him to look in her eyes.

"Johnnie," Brian said. "Johnnie True Blood. I was with Johnnie."

He looked deeply into Barbara's eyes. Barbara stared back into the eyes of this man who held her as he once had so many years before. He was the same man that he was then, but somehow, now he was so different. But, was he back to her? Was he sane? Alone in the woods for the night to commit suicide, and then talk of Johnnie True Blood?

"Johnnie is dead," Barbara said softly with a cautious querulous look.

"Yeah, yeah, I know."

Brian looked back over his shoulder down the dark trail momentarily lit by the morning sun, and raised his right hand. He looked back to Barbara, and smiled.

"Look Barb," he kissed her on the forehead. "I'm <u>not</u> nuts. God am I not nuts. We're gonna' be fine."

He took a deep breath.

"The things I could tell you..."

His hand moved from the dark shadow behind him into the light of day. He looked down at his right hand, and opened it revealing a single, gray dog tag. His palm was flat offering the dog tag, its indented letters colored dark brown with blood, to Barbara. The metal glowed light red.

Barbara's fingers slipped across the imprinted letters and numbers on the metal not needing to read with her eyes the name "Johnnie True Blood, NG 26869933, A Pos."

"I believe you," Barbara said.

Together, Brian and Barbara clasped their right hands around the legacy of Johnnie True Blood. Barbara slipped her hands beneath

Brian's shirt. Her fingertips glided across his chest sensing smooth skin where scars had been.

"Brian?"

Barbara pushed Brian gently back to see his eyes. His grin from an earlier time remained. Barbara shook her head to clear her eyes.

"Brian," she said softly.

"Yeah," Brian said. "It's me."

He held her tightly. Barbara felt at peace; a sensation she had not known in a very long time. Barbara cried, and the cries became sobs.

"It's all right, Barb, it's really all right," Brian said.

"Yes," Barbara said gently pushing back from Brian and looking up into his eyes.

"You're home. You're really, really home. I know that."

She cried hard, waved to Brian as she sought words, and then spoke.

"Thank you, Johnnie, thank you."

Brian looked at Henry Two Pines who was approaching them.

"You knew," said Brian nodding back toward the deep woods.

Henry Two Pines nodded.

"You knew all along."

"There are some benefits to getting older. Welcome home, Brian."

The three of them got into the truck. They sat there for a moment without speaking, and then Henry Two Pines started the engine and they drove out of the parking lot. They drove back down the narrow track out of the dark woods, the roof of the truck reflecting the red glow of the sun.

Above them in the trees, a lone Blue Jay sat atop a tall pine watching them leave, then stepped from the branch into the warming morning air rising effortlessly on the currents, accompanied with the low, warm tone of laughter from the living, the dead, and the dreaming.

CHAPTER 12

TAP DANCING IN THE SHADOW OF DEATH

NO FEAR OF THE NIGHT

It was late afternoon when Brian stopped Henry Two Pine's old truck at the edge of the Tamarack Lodge parking lot. Brian looked at Barbara's van with its crushed side, then to Barbara, and squeezed her hand.

"If something had happened to..."

Barbara's voice exploded into laughter startling Brian. She put her hand to her mouth.

"Jesus, Brian," she cried laughing and gasping for air. "I'm going to pee my pants."

She gasped for air trying to control herself. Then, she put her arms around Brian's neck pulling him to her.

"Oh lover, if something had happened to me? After all you, we've been through? You are back to me."

Quietly, Barbara sobbed pressing her head into Brian's collar. Looking up, she noticed Brian staring through the windshield. He nodded, blinked, moving his gaze from left to right across the parking lot.

Barbara watched Brian squint, his eyes mist, and his jaw clench. Brian turned, noticing Barbara's gaze upon him, and partially opened his mouth, but he had no words. He looked back to the parking lot still clutching Barbara's hand. She pressed two fingers to his lips. Barbara's eyebrows arched. She paused, and then looked to Brian, and then through the windshield following his gaze.

Bright clouds slid across the background of the bright sky. The breeze tossed the tops of tall pines. The lone Blue Jay circled above, spiraled down, and perched on a dead limb of a tall, majestic pine.

The bold stillness of the Adirondacks came upon Brian and Barbara at this moment. There are few moments in a lifetime when it can happen and it doesn't happen to all. Only to ones who have paid the price and earned a chance for the moment. It all stopped. No sound of wind in the trees. No movement of clouds. Their hearts beat to the same rhythm. No past. No present. No future.

Brian remembered what Johnnie True Blood had said to him. "You really can't stop things the way they were, and you couldn't stop Jenkins from moving on."

Brian stared with respect to the cavalry trooper standing in the parking lot of the Tamarack Lodge. It was the same trooper that Brian had seen the day before on his way north. Brian grinned broadly as Jenkins stepped into view. Brian looked to Barbara.

She nodded to Brian, looked through the windshield, saw pebbles move across the parking lot, and then saw the entire assembled host through Brian's eyes.

THE END

EPILOGUE

I'm Henry Two Pines, and I told you when it started that this story had to happen up here in the Adirondacks. There's a bold stillness that can come upon you up here, and change who you are for the better. It sure happened to Brian. Looking up to the Milky Way standing by the fire, and seeing that bright corridor of stars leading off across the sky. It's all so much bigger than you are. Katie did fine what with the operation and part of Brian's liver. Barbara and the newborn are fine. Brian's home, he's back, and he's living in the light. And, that's what this story is about.*

ABOUT THE AUTHOR

George Samerjan is a published poet, novelist, screen writer, and combat veteran. In 2002, he, and co-author David Saperstein, wrote the screenplay for A CHRISTMAS VISITOR which has aired on the Hallmark Channel annually since then, and around the world. In 2004, he co-wrote the novel of A CHRISTMAS VISITOR, and this was followed by A CHRISTMAS PASSAGE in 2008. LONG WAY HOME - The divine rescue of Sergeant McAfee from the demons of his war - and FROM THE SHADOWS - A young man overcomes family tragedy to heal himself and a veteran - were published as e-books in 2013. George Samerjan has written more than 2,000 poems and those poems have appeared in numerous publications.

His honors and awards include two Bronze Star Medals one with one Oak Leaf Cluster and one with "V" device, the Air Medal, Combat Infantryman Badge, Army Commendation Medal, Vietnamese Cross of Gallantry with Bronze Star, Vietnam Service Medal with Three Bronze Service Stars, and the Republic of Vietnam Campaign Medal.

He received an Emmy Award for Outstanding Achievement "Interactive Video Disc" in the Best Training or Information Program

Under Fifteen Minutes category. He is a member of the Writers Guild of America.

He is a life member of the Disabled Veterans of America, and the Combat Infantrymen's Association.

Other Books by this Author:

From The Shadows

(With David Saperstein)
A Christmas Visitor
A Christmas Passage

www.ingramcontent.com/pod-product-compliance
Lightning Source LLC
Chambersburg PA
CBHW020510030426
42337CB00011B/324